GERMAN HIGH SEAS FLEET 1914–18

The Kaiser's challenge to the Royal Navy

Angus Konstam
Illustrated by Edouard A. Groult

OSPREY PUBLISHING
Bloomsbury Publishing Plc
Kemp House, Chawley Park, Cumnor Hill, Oxford OX2 9PH, UK
29 Earlsfort Terrace, Dublin 2, Ireland
1385 Broadway, 5th Floor, New York, NY 10018, USA
E-mail: info@ospreypublishing.com
www.ospreypublishing.com

OSPREY is a trademark of Osprey Publishing Ltd

First published in Great Britain in 2023

A catalogue record for this book is available from the British Library.

ISBN: PB 9781472856470; eBook 9781472856456; ePDF 9781472856449; XML 9781472856463

23 24 25 26 27   10 9 8 7 6 5 4 3 2 1

Maps by bounford.com
Diagrams by Adam Tooby
Battlescenes by Edouard A. Groult
Index by Janet Andrew
Typeset by Myriam Bell Design
Printed and bound in India by Replika Press Private Ltd.

Front Cover: Art by Edouard A. Groult, © Osprey Publishing
Photographs: All photos in this book are courtesy of the Stratford Archive.

Osprey Publishing supports the Woodland Trust, the UK's leading woodland conservation charity.

To find out more about our authors and books visit www.ospreypublishing.com. Here you will find
extracts, author interviews, details of forthcoming events and the option to sign up for our newsletter.

CONTENTS

THE FLEET'S PURPOSE

On 23 June 1914, a British squadron arrived in Kiel to take part in Kiel Week, a naval gathering attended by Kaiser Wilhelm II. Participants spoke of the spirit of friendship between the British and German navies, and toasts to mutual comradeship were exchanged. It also gave the *Kaiserliche Marine* (Imperial German Navy) the chance to demonstrate its new-found naval strength, and, as *Vizeadmiral* (Vice Admiral) Reinhard von Scheer put it, 'an opportunity to make comparisons which were not in our disfavour'.

Just five days later, on 28 June, word reached Kiel that the Austrian heir-apparent Archduke Franz Ferdinand had been assassinated. The Kaiser left hurriedly to confer with his ministers, and two days later the British squadron would leave too, after offering parting words of eternal friendship. Five weeks later, on 4 August, Britain and Germany would be at war with each other, and their two fleets would be mortal enemies. Although a number of Germany's light warships were scattered around the globe, the bulk of its naval strength was concentrated into the *Hochseeflotte* (High Seas Fleet), which was designed to operate in the North Sea. This stretch of water would thus become the key naval battleground between this powerful German fleet and its British counterpart, the Grand Fleet. It was possible that the fates of both countries would rest on the performance of their battle fleets.

The very creation of the High Seas Fleet in 1907 had been part of a naval stratagem, 'the Risk Theory', which argued that a powerful German fleet would deter Britain from intervening in Germany's rise to imperial power, the Kaiser's ambition. If the two fleets clashed, it was probable that the larger Grand Fleet would be the victor. The key to the stratagem was to ensure that any war would result in such a costly, pyrrhic victory for the British that the Royal Navy would lose its naval dominance, which in turn would leave it dangerously vulnerable to other, smaller rivals. Given such a strategic scenario, Britain would choose to protect its navy and empire, and decline to fight Germany. The role of the

High Seas Fleet was not to fight its way to predominance, but rather to hold the status of the Royal Navy hostage.

When war came, however, not only did the British avoid this decisive, costly battle until mid-1916, but they came within an ace of destroying the High Seas Fleet. The British also used geography to render the German fleet ineffective, through its inability to defeat the Grand Fleet and break Britain's economic blockade of Germany. Ultimately, this blockade would ensure an Allied victory in the war, and the surrender en masse of the High Seas Fleet. The outcome of the naval war could have been very different if the High Seas Fleet had been able to achieve its quickly re-designed mission: whittling down the strength of the Grand Fleet piecemeal until the naval balance gave Germany the edge in the North Sea. Then, *Der Tag* would have come when the High Seas Fleet could show its worth.

THE KAISER'S 'LUXURY FLEET'

Many historical fleets had a clear mission, or a role which they were built to fulfil. The High Seas Fleet never really enjoyed this clarity of purpose. Instead, it was created out of political desire, and its existence made possible because of a revolution in naval technology. It was called upon to fulfil a mission which in all probability had ceased to serve any real purpose before the coming of war in August 1914. Unlike most other maritime powers, the German economy did not rely primarily on maritime trade, and its relatively short coastline contained just a handful of major ports. Nor did it have extensive overseas colonies. Germany had no real need for a powerful seagoing fleet. Yet when war began, the High Seas Fleet was second only to its British counterpart in terms of size, power and fighting potential.

In June 1888 Kaiser (Emperor) Wilhelm II acceded to the German throne, following the death earlier that year of both his father and grandfather. The 29-year-old was more headstrong than his predecessors, and more aggressive in international affairs. He was also determined to turn Germany into a maritime

The dreadnought SMS *König*, the namesake of what was until 1916 the most modern class of dreadnoughts in the High Seas Fleet, and the flagship of Battle Squadron III at Jutland. This was a superbly designed vessel, with armour and underwater protection of a quality that greatly impressed the British on their examination of the ship after the war.

power, and he devoured Alfred Mahan's *The Influence of Sea Power Upon History* (1890), which stressed the importance of naval power on national standing. This avenue, together with colonial expansion, would be Wilhelm's route to establishing Germany as a world power.

Germany already had a small navy, the *Kaiserliche Marine*. Founded in 1871, it was essentially a coastal defence force. When the new Kaiser ascended the throne, work had already begun on the Kaiser Wilhelm Canal, linking the Baltic to the North Sea, and on the establishment of naval bases at Kiel and Wilhelmshaven. This became the new Kaiser's starting point for his naval expansion.

Wilhelm set about securing funds for his naval project and enlarging his fleet, starting with a class of small coastal defence battleships. However, this expansion lacked direction until 1897, when *Konteradmiral* (Rear Admiral) Alfred von Tirpitz (1849–1930) became the new Secretary of State for the Navy. As early as 1892, Tirpitz had drawn up a strategic plan for the *Kaiserliche Marine*, in an attempt to steer the Kaiser towards the building of a battle fleet, together with a cruiser force to support colonial ventures overseas. It was Tirpitz who, in 1898, secured the funds the Kaiser needed for his next stage of naval expansion. It turned out that the admiral, who had never heard a gun fired in anger, was a natural when it came to fighting the navy's corner in Germany's political arena.

The result was the rapid expansion of the navy, and, in 1900, Tirpitz secured the funds to dramatically increase the size of the battle fleet over the next two decades. This caused significant concern in Britain, as German motives were rightly questioned. It also coincided with a wave of anti-British feeling in Germany, the result of Germany's affinity for the rebels in the Second Boer War (1899–1902). This mutual suspicion between the two countries laid the groundwork for the naval arms race that would follow.

In early 1912, Winston Churchill, Britain's new First Lord of the Admiralty, dismissed the need for a powerful German fleet. He said: 'We have never had any thoughts of aggression.' He then stressed the difference between the two naval powers:

> The British Navy is to us a necessity, and, from some points of view, the German Navy is to them more in the nature of a luxury. Our naval power involves British existence. It is existence to us; it is expansion to them… The whole fortunes of our race and Empire, the whole treasure accumulated during so many centuries of sacrifice and achievement, would perish and be swept utterly away if our naval supremacy were to be impaired.

This was Britain's answer to German naval expansion: Britain was determined to maintain its naval supremacy in order to maintain its empire, which was bound together by maritime trade.

The First Lord also emphasized the foolhardiness of attempting to rival British naval power: 'Instead of overtaking us by additional efforts, [you] will only be more out-distanced in consequence of the measures which we ourselves shall take.' In other words, Britain was determined to maintain its naval supremacy, regardless of the cost, as it was seen as the bedrock of British prosperity. Despite this, though, Germany continued to indulge in the naval arms race, notwithstanding the economic and diplomatic consequences. Churchill had labelled the German Navy as a 'luxury fleet', an expensive folly built purely to satisfy Germany's national ego. With no major overseas colonies to defend, and a relatively small national coastline, it seemed there was little strategic need for a High Seas Fleet. Indeed, as far as Churchill and others could see, its sole *raison d'être* was to challenge Britain, a country which, before 1914, had been regarded as a natural ally. The German viewpoint was markedly different. For them, it was simply a matter of deterrence.

The creation of a large, powerful Imperial German fleet was designed primarily to increase Germany's standing in the world. From the start it never had any really clear *raison d'être*. (From the oil painting by Claus Bergen, *High Seas Fleet Setting Sail, 31 May 1916*)

THE RISK THEORY

Tirpitz claimed he had no real desire to go to war with Britain. For him, the building up of a powerful battleship force was part of his own strategic plan. While he might not want a war with Britain, he saw the Royal Navy as his new fleet's most likely potential adversary. He even told the Kaiser: 'For Germany, the most dangerous naval enemy at present is England.' It was clear that ultimately the ability to challenge Britain's naval supremacy was his strategic objective. He realized, however, that it could take almost two decades to build a fleet of the size he required to take on the British. In the meantime, until the *Kaiserliche Marine* grew large enough, Tirpitz had to modify his strategic goals, and therefore he developed his own doctrine which suited the situation Germany found itself in. He would call it his *Risikogedanke* (Risk Theory).

Admiral von Tirpitz developed his Risk Theory as his own adaptation of Mahan's thesis on sea power. This would be the policy which lay behind the creation of the High Seas Fleet, and would govern its strategic precepts. Ultimately, it would lead to the great naval clash at Jutland in 1916. The Risk Theory required the existence of a large German battle fleet, made up of the most modern and powerful battleships the country could produce. In the event of a war with 'a superior naval power', the size and power of the German fleet would act as a deterrent to the enemy power, who would logically see a decisive naval battle against Germany as being prohibitively costly. Although the 'superior power' would probably win the battle, its losses would be so great that its power would be fatally weakened.

At that point, a third naval power, or even an alliance of more than one enemy, could more easily defeat what remained of the once-superior fleet. Thus, the Risk Theory centred on making any attack on the German fleet an unacceptable risk. Although he did not state it, there was no real doubt which 'superior fleet' Tirpitz was writing about. By adopting this naval stratagem, as Germany did in 1899, it was clear that tensions would inevitably increase between the two countries. This was fuelled too by the appearance of Germany's first new battleships of the Brandenburg class, launched from 1891 on. By late 1904, shortly before *Dreadnought* was laid down, there were 15 modern battleships in the *Kaiserliche Marine*, with more either nearing completion or about to be laid down. *Dreadnought*, though, would upset Tirpitz's carefully laid plans.

The launch of the revolutionary *Dreadnought* in February 1906 levelled the naval playing field. Overnight, the pre-dreadnought battle fleets of both nations were rendered obsolete. With ten 30.5cm (12in) guns, steam turbine propulsion and thick armour, *Dreadnought* was faster and more powerful than any warship afloat. Both nations would now have to start rebuilding their costly navies from scratch, and with Britain's much bigger fleet of capital ships now obsolete, this naval revolution offered a rare chance for Germany to challenge the Royal Navy. Undeterred, and fully supported by both the Kaiser and the Reichstag, Tirpitz embarked on an ambitious shipbuilding programme. This in turn led to the naval arms race that most historians consider was a major contributing factor in the outbreak of war between the two countries in August 1914.

For the British, the very fact that the Germans were willing to build their own powerful dreadnought fleet came as a surprise, given the immense cost involved, both in money and resources. This, though, merely increased the determination of the British to win the race. The first German dreadnought was launched in March 1908, two years after the original *Dreadnought*, and by late 1911 seven of these powerful German battleships were in service, compared to

Virtually overnight, the coming of the *Dreadnought* rendered Germany's existing battle fleet obsolete. Still, to have a chance of taking on their British counterparts, the High Seas Fleet had to incorporate a number of these vulnerable pre-dreadnought battleships. Their crews dubbed them *Fünf-Minuten-Schiffe* ('five-minute ships'), as that was how long they were expected to survive in a naval battle against dreadnoughts.

The SMS *Nassau*, namesake of the first class of four German dreadnoughts. In terms of armoured protection and propulsion they were well-designed, but were slightly let down by their relatively small-calibre main battery of 28cm (11in) guns and their awkward turret configuration, where only four of the six turrets could fire on any single beam.

ten British ones. At that point the British redoubled their efforts, and began to increase the gap between the two fleets. Consequently, by August 1914, 17 German dreadnoughts and battlecruisers would be matched by 29 British ones, with the British also having more under construction than their rivals. It was this imbalance – one that would increase as the war continued – that would increasingly call into question the efficacy of the Risk Theory.

FORCE BALANCING

During the weeks leading to the outbreak of war, both Tirpitz and the Kaiser clung to the hope that the Risk Theory had paid off, but it soon became clear that the whole premise had been undermined: not in the shipyards but around the negotiating tables. For the Risk Theory to work, it required other naval powers to be able and willing to challenge the global supremacy of the Royal Navy. Instead, Britain joined France and Russia in the anti-German alliance,[1] and although that still left the major naval powers of Japan, Italy and the United States neutral, they too would eventually side with the Allies in 1914, 1915 and 1917 respectively. Only Austria-Hungary sided with Germany, and its own small battle fleet was effectively countered by the entry of Italy into the war.

Therefore, even if the British battle fleet was gravely weakened in a naval campaign in the North Sea, no third power would take advantage of this to challenge British naval supremacy. The entry of the United States into the war

---

1   This element of the Risk Theory had already been undermined since the turn of the century, with the Anglo-Japanese Alliance signed in 1902 and the Entente Cordiale of 1904 with France. These alliances reduced Britain's need to maintain heavy naval forces in the Mediterranean and the China Station, and allowed it to concentrate its forces in the Grand Fleet.

Grossadmiral Alfred von Tirpitz (1849–1930) was a skilled administrator and political lobbyist who spearheaded the financing of a German battle fleet and oversaw its creation. During the war he became disillusioned by the lack of a suitable role for the High Seas Fleet, and so turned to the U-boat as the solution to Germany's strategic problems.

in April 1917 was the final nail in the Risk Theory's coffin. From 1916, President Wilson realized that the victors would be in a position to threaten America's global interests, so his government embarked on a major shipbuilding programme designed to achieve naval parity with Britain. By war's end, the *Kaiserliche Marine* would no longer be the world's second-largest fleet.

The Risk Theory also required the British to send their battle fleet into the North Sea to maintain a tight economic blockade of the German coast. Instead, Britain's Grand Fleet used geography to its advantage, and opted for a distant blockade. By bottling up the English Channel, and by stationing the Grand Fleet at Scapa Flow in Orkney, there was no need for the British to place their fleet in harm's way and, consequently, the hugely expensive High Seas Fleet was condemned to strategic inaction. All that was left to Germany was a very limited version of their plan, which involved attempting to tempt out elements of the Grand Fleet and to bring it to battle on advantageous terms. This stratagem was known as the *Kräfteausgleich* (Force Balancing). While the German fleet awaited the opportunity to ambush its opponents, Tirpitz himself abandoned his belief that the battle fleet was the arbiter of victory at sea. Instead, he became an advocate of unrestricted U-boat warfare.

Tirpitz, now a *Grossadmiral* (Grand Admiral), had never done much about building up the U-boat arm of his fleet. Instead, he had emphasized the use of torpedo boats to whittle down the enemy battle fleet through *Kräfteausgleich* before a decisive surface battle was fought. By 1915 he had become an advocate of the U-boat, and saw its potential in wreaking economic damage on Britain by preying on her maritime trade routes. In the end, his support for unrestricted U-boat warfare would lead to his fall from grace with the Kaiser, and would ultimately result in his resignation from office in March 1916.

Instead, it was left to the commanders of the High Seas Fleet to make the most of the still-powerful naval tools at their disposal. The policy of whittling down the British Grand Fleet had merit, but as the imbalance between the two fleets increased, this became an increasingly risky stratagem. As a result, at Jutland, after the High Seas Fleet narrowly avoided defeat, the policy of whittling down the enemy was abandoned. Instead, apart from the occasional defensive sortie, the High Seas Fleet became a 'fleet in being', a Mahanian concept which saw its ships serving to tie down larger numbers of the enemy fleet, in case it would make a sortie. This became the fleet's final stratagem – its survival as a powerful fighting entity until the war was decided by other, terrestrial means.

FLEET FIGHTING POWER

THE SHIPS

Dreadnoughts

The *Kaiserliche Marine*'s first dreadnoughts, or 'super battleships' as the Germans first called them, were the four vessels of the Nassau class. These had been designed by the navy's chief architect Hans Bürkner, and laid down in secret during the summer of 1907. They entered service three years later. Bürkner placed greater emphasis on protection than speed or armament, and this established a path that would be followed by the fleet's subsequent dreadnoughts. They used conventional reciprocating engines rather than the steam turbines used in *Dreadnought*, so these ships were slower than their British counterparts. Their 28cm (11in) guns were of a smaller calibre too, while the space taken up by machinery resulted in the ships' awkward turret configuration. As a result, despite carrying 12 guns, they only had double the broadside firepower of their pre-dreadnought forebears.

The next group, the three-funnel Helgoland class, represented an improvement. Internal space was better arranged, and although they shared the same problem with turret layout, they carried 30.5cm (12in) guns, had better underwater protection and were slightly faster. Although still coal-powered, auxiliary oil burners were installed in 1915.[2] These entered service in 1911–12. The subsequent five-ship Kaiser class represented a significant leap forward. Not only were they fitted with steam turbines, giving them a slightly greater speed than their predecessors, but their 30.5cm guns were mounted on the centreline or echeloned amidships, which offered a greater broadside capability, despite carrying one turret fewer. They were also better protected, with a belt up to 35cm (14in) thick. These dreadnoughts entered service in 1913.

---

2   As fuel oil had to be imported, and coal was available in German Silesia, there was a strategic preference for a fuel which was home-produced.

The four König-class dreadnoughts which followed were similar, but enjoyed a much better turret layout, with only one centreline turret amidships, and two centreline turrets fore and aft, one superfiring over the other. Better gun elevation also meant increased range. The final dreadnoughts to join the fleet (although more had been planned) were the two Bayern-class 'super dreadnoughts' which were laid down before the war, and which entered service in 1916–17. These mounted eight 38cm (15in) guns in four twin turrets – two forward and two aft, with one superfiring over the other. Although not especially better armoured or faster than the previous German dreadnoughts, their firepower was equivalent to that of the Grand Fleet's 'fast battleships', only with better protection and less speed.

The weak points in the German battle fleet were the pre-dreadnought battleships, which the commanders of the High Seas Fleet had to rely on to offset the numerical superiority of their British opponents. There was nothing particularly impressive about the Braunschweig or Deutschland classes. One of the former took part in Jutland, together with all of the Deutschland class, where their slow speed and relative lack of both protection and firepower rendered them something of a liability. One of them, *Pommern*, was sunk during the battle, the victim of a torpedo fired by a British destroyer. As a result, the remaining pre-dreadnoughts were withdrawn from the High Seas Fleet towards the end of 1916, as the addition of the new Bayerns more than compensated for their loss.

The Scouting Groups

Germany's first battlecruiser, *Von der Tann*, was laid down in Hamburg in early 1908, and joined the High Seas Fleet three years later. Although the British move towards battlecruisers was the impetus for the ship's construction, *Von der Tann* was a much better-designed warship than British contemporaries. While *Von der Tann* only carried eight 28cm (11in) guns, their layout meant they could all fire a broadside and, with an armoured belt 25cm (10in) thick, the battlecruiser was much better protected too. Although badly battered at Jutland, *Von der Tann* remained afloat thanks to having a superior watertight sub-division, a feature

Two König-class dreadnoughts of the German battle fleet pictured while on exercise off the German coast, escorted by a brace of torpedo boats. (From the oil painting by Claus Bergen, *German Battleships Passing Helgoland*)

The battlecruiser SMS *Seydlitz* at sea, pictured late in the war from the deck of a torpedo boat. Seen here clearly running at speed, as the stern is digging into the water. Like other German battlecruisers *Seydlitz* could make over 26 knots, but that still made the battlecruiser slightly slower than the generation of British battlecruisers dubbed the 'Splendid Cats'.

the ship shared with all subsequent German battlecruisers. In their duel, *Von der Tann*'s guns also blew up *Indefatigable*.

The two Moltke-class battlecruisers which followed were larger than *Von der Tann*, with an armament of ten 28cm guns, the after pair in a superfiring configuration, and with a slightly thicker armoured belt. Of the two ships in the class, *Moltke* and *Goeben*, only *Moltke* served with the High Seas Fleet. Both entered service in 1912. They were followed by *Seydlitz*, a slightly enlarged version of the previous class. Essentially though, there was little difference between these ships.

Their successors of the Derfflinger class represented a significant step forward. They were flush-decked, and their 30.5cm (12in) guns were mounted on the centreline fore and aft, in a superfiring configuration. Although their protective belt was no thicker than their predecessors', it was more extensive. This did not prevent *Lützow* succumbing to uncontrolled flooding after Jutland, following at least 24 large-calibre hits, but ship for ship the Derfflingers were markedly superior to their British counterparts. What let the German battlecruisers down slightly was that, like the dreadnoughts, they lacked the larger-calibre guns and turn of speed available to their enemy counterparts.

At Jutland it was *Derfflinger* that blew up the *Queen Mary*, while *Lützow* did the same to *Invincible*. *Derfflinger* entered service in November 1914, but it was another 16 months before *Lützow* was commissioned, just two months before Jutland. The same basic design was followed in the last German battlecruiser to join the fleet. *Hindenburg* was a slightly enlarged version of the Derfflingers, with more graceful hull lines, and joined the fleet in October 1917.

Little needs to be said of the High Seas Fleet's light cruisers, which had a fairly straightforward lineage. Unlike the British, who distinguished between commerce protection cruisers and fleet reconnaissance ones, the Germans combined the two roles into one type of cruiser, used in the battle fleet as well as for trade protection and commerce raiding. This compromise led to larger but slightly slower cruisers than the British ones. The international trend was to build larger, better-protected and better-armed vessels, and following the introduction of steam turbines cruisers were faster too. The Germans were slow to adopt the 15cm (6in) gun, which first appeared in the Pillau class that entered service in 1914–15. Before that the 10.5cm (4.1in) gun was the norm, and from 1916 on most of the surviving earlier cruisers were rearmed.

At the start of the war a number of armoured cruisers were in service, although by 1907 when *Blücher* was laid down, it was already clear that this was a ship type which had been superseded by the battlecruiser. Armoured cruisers simply lacked the speed, protection and firepower needed to be of much value in combat. In 1914 the only armoured cruiser in the High Seas Fleet was *Blücher*, completed in 1910 and lost at Dogger Bank (1915), where the faults of her flawed design were exposed.

From the start, German torpedo boats were designed to operate in support of the battle fleet, which meant they had to be larger than the torpedo vessels currently in vogue with other European navies. While the British emphasized the need for their equivalent vessels to be able to protect the fleet, this was of secondary importance to German designers. Instead, the function of these

TACTICAL METHODS: DEPLOYMENT OF SCOUTING FORCES, MAY 1916

During the sortie towards the Skagerrak that resulted in the battle of Jutland, Vizeadmiral Hipper's Scouting Forces were deployed approximately 50nm ahead of Vizeadmiral Scheer's battle fleet. They had two roles. The first was to scout ahead of the fleet, and to warn Scheer if elements of the British Grand Fleet were at sea. If they encountered the British Battlecruiser Fleet, they were to draw them south again, towards Scheer's dreadnoughts. Then the enemy could be destroyed between the two German forces. If the British were not encountered, then on reaching the Skagerrak, Hipper's Scouting Group was to sweep through it to the east, sinking and destroying any Allied ships they encountered.

This shows the formation of Hipper's Scouting Forces as they steamed north in the early afternoon of 31 May 1916 – shortly before they encountered the lead elements of Beatty's fleet. The five battlecruisers of the 1st Scouting Group form the core of the force, deployed in line astern, with Hipper's flagship *Lützow* in the lead. It is screened by the 11 torpedo boats (destroyers) of Flotilla IX. Stationed seven miles ahead of *Lützow* is the light cruiser *Frankfurt*, flagship of Konteradmiral Bödicker, commander of 2nd Scouting Group. His other three light cruisers (*Elbing*, *Pillau* and *Wiesbaden*) are on station either five or ten miles from the flagship, as

is the light cruiser *Regensburg*, flagship of Kommodore Heinrich, commanding Hipper's torpedo boat forces. With visibility in the North Sea around 12–15 miles that day, that gave Bödicker a scouting coverage of up to 50nm.

Each of the five cruisers is screened by a cluster of torpedo boats, from Flotillas II and VI. In theory, each of these flotillas consisted of 11 vessels – the flotilla leader, then two half-flotillas of five boats each. However, one half-flotilla from Flotilla VI only had three torpedo boats, while another half-flotilla from Flotilla II was one vessel short. The positions of the three flotilla leaders are marked, Flotilla II commanded by Kapitän Schuur in *B-98*, Flotilla VI by Kapitän Schultz in *G-41* and Flotilla IX by Kapitän Goehle in *V-28*.

That afternoon, contact with the enemy was first made by the torpedo boat *B-98*, accompanying the *Elbing*, on the far western end of the line. A merchant steamer had been spotted, and Kapitän Madung of the *Elbing* sent the torpedo boats *B-98* and *B-110* to investigate. As they did so they spotted funnel smoke to the west, and at 1520hrs two British cruisers were spotted – *Galatea* and *Phaeton*. *Elbing* had altered course to the west too, and spotted the enemy ships at 1531, opening fire a minute later at a range of 14,000m. This was the opening shot of the battle of Jutland.

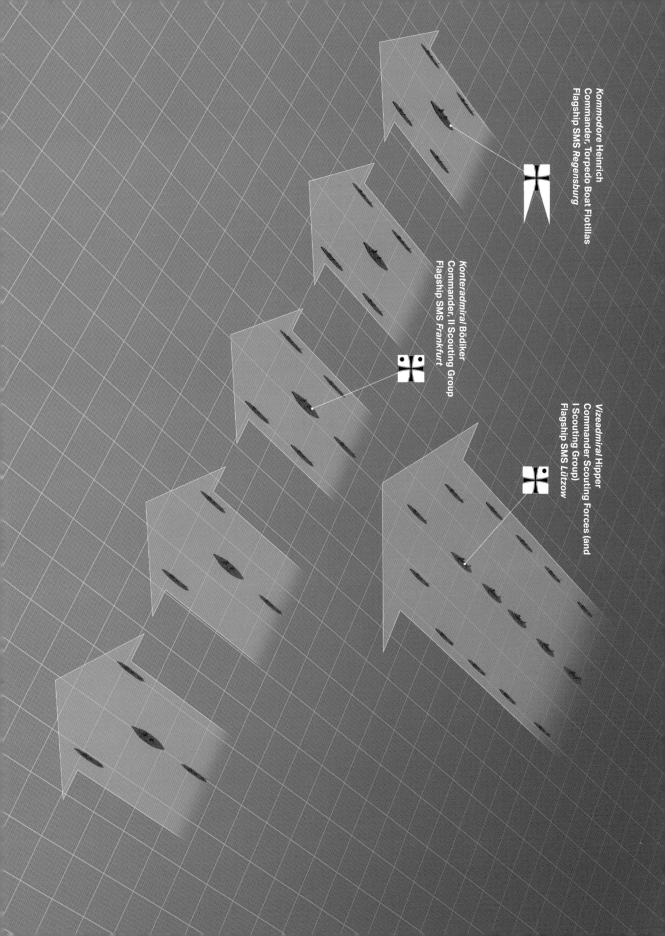

Kommodore Heinrich
Commander, Torpedo Boat Flotillas
Flagship SMS *Regensburg*

Konteradmiral Bödiker
Commander, II Scouting Group
Flagship SMS *Frankfurt*

Vizeadmiral Hipper
Commander Scouting Forces (and I Scouting Group)
Flagship SMS *Lützow*

In the Dogger Bank operation in January 1915 the armoured cruiser SMS *Blücher* was something of a liability to Hipper and his Scouting Group I, being slower than the battlecruisers and lacking their armour and protection. As a result, *Blücher* fell easy victim to Beatty's faster and better-armed battlecruisers.

CHANGES TO THE HIGH SEAS FLEET, 1914–18

March 1917: *Bayern* becomes fleet flagship

Battle Squadron I Active throughout the war	No changes
Battle Squadron II Active until December 1916, then inactive	*Pommern* lost at Jutland, 1 June 1916
Battle Squadron III Active throughout the war	*Grosser Kurfürst* joins V Division
	February 1915: with exception *of Grosser Kurfürst*, V Division is redesignated as VI Division; V Division now comprises *König* (flag, Konteradmiral Behnke), *Kronprinz*, *Markgraf* and *Grosser Kurfurst*
	July 1916: *Bayern* joins V Division
	December 1916: VI Division transferred to IV Battle Squadron
Battle Squadron IV Active from December 1916 until end of war (*Konteradmiral* Mauve)	VI Division (Mauve): *Prinzregent Luitpold* (flag), *Kaiser*, *Kaiserin*, *König Albert*
	March 1917: *Friedrich der Grosse* joins VI Division
1st Scouting Group Active throughout the war	*Blücher* lost at Dogger Bank, 24 January 1915
	Lützow lost at Jutland, 1 June 1916
	May 1917: *Hindenburg* joins the SG
2nd Scouting Group Active throughout the war	Losses: *Köln* and *Mainz* lost at Helgoland, 28 August 1914, *Elbing*, *Rostock* and *Wiesbaden* lost at Jutland, 31 May–1 June 1916
	Reinforcements: *Graudenz* (September 1914), *Regensburg* (April 1915), *Frankfurt* and *Wiesbaden* (August 1915), *Elbing* (September 1915), *Pillau* (December 1915), *Konigsberg ii* (August 1916), *Karlsruhe ii* and *Nürnberg ii* (November 1916), *Emden ii* (December 1916), *Köln ii* (January 1918), *Dresden ii* (March 1918)
	Transfers: *Kolberg* to Baltic (June 1915), *Stralsund* and *Strassburg* to 4th SG (March 1916), *Regensburg* to 4th SG (July 1917), *Frankfurt* to 4th SG (August 1918)
3rd Scouting Group (4th SG from August 1914) Active throughout the war	25 August 1914: redesignated as 4th Scouting Group
	Losses: *Hela* lost off Helgoland, 13 September 1914, *Frauenlob* lost at Jutland, 31 May 1916
	Reinforcements: *Stettin* (August 1914), *Stralsund* (March 1916), *Brummer* (April 1916), *Bremse* (July 1916), *Regensburg* (July 1917), *Strassburg* (April 1918), *Frankfurt* (August 1918)
	Transfers: *Stuttgart* (May 1916) *Danzig* and *München* (December 1916), *Stettin* (July 1917)
4th Scouting Group (3rd SG from August 1914) Active until March 1915	25 August 1914: redesignated as 3rd Scouting Group
	September 1914: *Friedrich Karl* transferred to Baltic – lost there in November 1914
	Yorck lost on Jade Estuary, 4 November 1914
	March 1915: 4th SG transferred to Baltic, then deactivated

torpedo boats was to conduct large-scale torpedo attacks against the enemy battle fleet, in support of their own battleships. In response, the British developed the destroyer, a small warship with the firepower to drive off enemy torpedo boat attacks, and with a secondary torpedo armament. The Germans placed their emphasis on torpedo armament, speed and seaworthiness.

German torpedo boat designs evolved during the years preceding World War I, but essentially they were built around their torpedo armament of up to six tubes, mounted singly or in 'V-shaped' paired mounts, carrying 50cm (19.7in) torpedoes. For the *Kaiserliche Marine*, torpedo attacks were seen as a key element in the fleet commander's repertoire, and the primary means of whittling down the numerical advantage enjoyed by the British in terms of capital ships. In practice, however, torpedo attacks appear to have been less effective than anticipated, largely due to the problems inherent in coordinating them during a naval engagement.

TECHNOLOGY

The Germans had done their best to keep up with the rapidly changing technologies of the past decade. By 1914 their battle fleet was the second most powerful force of its kind in the world, and arguably the most advanced. In terms of size, even the United States Navy, with its ten dreadnoughts, had been

THE SCOUTING GROUP AT WILHELMSHAVEN, PREPARING TO PUT TO SEA, AUGUST 1914 (overleaf)

The German naval base of Wilhelmshaven lay on the western side of the Jade Bight, a bay on Germany's North Sea coast. Access from the port to the open sea was by means of the Jade Estuary, a channel flanked by mudflats and banks. So, naval units putting to sea from the port tended to form up in the Jade Roads, to the east of the port, before steaming northwards through the Jade towards the open sea. Early on the morning of Friday, 28 August 1914, the German light cruisers and torpedo boats on patrol around the North Sea island of Helgoland were surprised and attacked by a larger British force of cruisers. Helgoland covered the approaches to the Jade, and so reinforcements were called for to support the patrol line. This scene shows these reinforcements lying in the Jade Roads, at 0700hrs that morning. They are preparing to get underway to join the fight, which is taking place 40 miles to the north.

In the foreground the light cruiser *Köln* flies the flag of the Scouting Group commander, Konteradmiral (Rear Admiral) Maas. Accompanying him are the two larger and more modern Magdeburg-class light cruisers, *Strassburg* and *Stralsund*. In the background is the main entrance to Wilhelmshaven, home of the German High Seas Fleet. The rising smoke is from the force of German battlecruisers preparing to follow Maas to sea, but the departure of these heavy ships would have to wait until high tide.

In what became known as the battle of Helgoland Bight – the first major naval clash of the war – Maas would join the fight, but shortly before noon he would be ambushed by a force of British battlecruisers. In the confused skirmish that followed *Köln* would be sunk, and Maas killed.

overtaken by Imperial Germany, a situation exacerbated by financial constraints in the US. Tirpitz, though, had fewer limitations thanks to the support of the Kaiser and, to a large extent, the support of the German people. He also had some of the finest industrial companies in the world at his disposal. This in turn influenced the pace with which new technologies in ordnance, armour production, optics and wireless were adopted by the *Kaiserliche Marine*.

Armour

The ability of a warship to survive an attack was part of the trinity of warship design during this period – protection, propulsion and firepower – but for the *Kaiserliche Marine* it remained the dominant element. After all, the High Seas Fleet was designed to fight within a few hundred miles of its own bases; therefore good protection against gunfire or torpedoes helped ensure that these immensely expensive vessels were given the best possible chance to return home, and so live to fight another day. While protection against gunfire was provided by steel armour plate, a combination of multi-layered hull sides and double bottoms provided defence against underwater detonations from mines and torpedoes. German warship designers also made extensive use of watertight bulkheads, to divide the ship into sealable compartments that would help to contain any flooding.

During the operations of the High Seas Fleet, the protection afforded to German capital ships helped ensure that for the most part, although battered, these ships managed to limp home. Much of that had to do with the type of armour used in major German warships, and in the emphasis German designers placed on internal protection. In the case of armour, the *Kaiserliche Marine* adopted a similar approach to other naval powers. Armoured protection for a contemporary capital ship resembled a long steel box, known as the citadel, which protected the vitals of the ship – its magazines and machinery spaces. Its sides were formed by an armoured belt running along the hull, its ends were sealed by transverse armoured bulkheads and its roof was formed by a thinner

The starboard side of the battlecruiser SMS *Derfflinger* pictured on return to Wilhelmshaven after the battle of Jutland. *Derfflinger* was hit at least 30 times during the battle, and all but four of the guns were knocked out. Still, thanks to the battlecruiser's armoured protection, *Derfflinger* made it home and returned to service in mid-October 1916.

armoured deck. Key items outside this citadel, such as gun turrets and barbettes, were also protected by armour plate.

Germany was fortunate to have one of the leading steel producers in the world at its disposal. The family firm of Krupp, based in Essen, first made its mark producing high-quality steel which armed the 19th-century forces of Prussia. In 1890 the company developed nickel steel, an iron-nickel alloy which dramatically improved the quality of contemporary steel plate, with a thinner plate providing better protection than a thicker steel plate produced by other methods. Until then the naval standard was Harvey armour, named after its American inventor. For a few years Krupp nickel steel enjoyed a qualitative edge, until their process was copied by others. By then, however, Krupp had developed a greatly improved steel, which would be used to protect the Kaiser's dreadnoughts.

Shortly after 1900, Krupp's scientists discovered that by slightly altering the composition of their steel alloy, and selectively hardening one side in Krupp's furnaces, the resulting steel plate was far more effective. Essentially it had a harder face, and a more flexible rear face, which reduced the chances of the plate splintering if hit by an enemy shell. This new type of steel, known as Krupp cemented steel, or 'KC armour', was therefore slightly more effective than the other forms of homogenous armour used by Germany's rivals. It was found, though, that KC armour was less effective than homogenous armour when warding off glancing, oblique hits. Accordingly, in the *Kaiserliche Marine*, deck armour was made from Krupp nickel steel.

What was notable about the capital ships of the High Seas Fleet was the way the emphasis German naval architects placed on protection was translated into warship design. The pre-dreadnoughts of the Braunschweig and Deutschland classes had KC armour belts 225mm thick, tapering to 160mm at either end. Their 35–40mm nickel-steel armoured decks were thinner than many contemporary battleships, but they employed the Böchung system of sloped armour at their outer ends, where the decks met the outer belt. This was typical of warships of the period, but the thinner decks were the result of a weight saving based on the premise that in a gunnery action the range would decrease rapidly, and therefore thicker deck armour was unnecessary. The battle of Dogger Bank in 1915 put paid to that notion.

Germany's first dreadnoughts were significantly better protected than their British contemporaries, with armour taking up 36 per cent of displacement, compared to 28 per cent in *Dreadnought*. The Nassau and Helgoland classes had KC armour belts 290–300mm thick, tapering towards either end, and an upper citadel belt 160–170mm thick. This compared favourably to their British counterparts. For the Kaiser, König and Bayern classes this belt was increased to 350mm, with a 200mm upper citadel, while the superstructure was also protected by 170mm of KC armour. All of these dreadnoughts employed the Böchung system, and the later classes had thicker armoured decks, up to 60mm in the Königs and Bayerns, which compared favourably to the latest British dreadnoughts.

The interior of a gun turret on a German König- or Kaiser-class dreadnought. After the Dogger Bank battle, improved safety measures were introduced to reduce the risk of opened powder cartridges igniting, causing flash fires to spread from turret to magazine. (From the oil painting by Claus Bergen, *Inside a Battleship Main Turret*)

During the battle of Jutland, the battlecruiser SMS *Seydlitz* was hit repeatedly, and 'C' turret, pictured here in the superfiring position behind 'D' turret, was knocked out. Improved safety measures, however, prevented a repeat of the catastrophic damage suffered by both turrets at Dogger Bank the year before. (From the oil painting by Claus Bergen, *SMS Seydlitz at the Skagerrak Battle*)

This same emphasis on protection was also extended to the battlecruiser fleet. Again, compared to British battlecruisers, these had roughly 10 per cent more of their total displacement devoted to armour, and consequently they were significantly better protected. The first of them, *Von der Tann*, had a 250mm belt of KC armour, and this increased to 270m and 300mm in the Moltkes and *Seydlitz* respectively. The Derfflingers and *Hindenburg* largely followed *Seydlitz*'s protection scheme, so even the earliest, *Von der Tann*, had an armoured belt 100mm (4in) thicker than the contemporary British Invincible-class ships. Effectively, in terms of protection, all of these battlecruisers were slightly lighter versions of the fleet's dreadnoughts. Their thicker armour, put to the test at Dogger Bank and Jutland, may well have saved Hipper from suffering greater losses.

The weak spot in all German dreadnoughts and battlecruisers, at least at first, was their deck armour. That lack of protection against plunging fire also extended to the roofs of gun turrets, although this was partially rectified in the later dreadnoughts. A much better degree of thought was devoted to underwater protection. All of these German capital ships had extensive double bottoms, covering as much as four-fifths of the ship, while they were also fitted with torpedo bulkheads. These consisted of an inner steel bulkhead about 40–50mm thick parallel to the ship's side, and set about 4m back from it. The void in between was divided into compartments, some of which were filled with coal. The idea was that if a torpedo struck the ship's hull below the waterline, this bulkhead would protect the vitals of the ship from flooding. Britain's pre-war capital ships lacked this key protective feature, which proved its worth several times during the war.

Gunnery and Fire Control

The weak point of German capital ship design was the relatively small calibre of their main armament. Where the *Kaiserliche Marine* opted for 28cm (11in) and 30.5cm (12in) guns, British ships mounted 12in guns in their earliest dreadnoughts and battlecruisers, and 13.5in (34.3cm) ones in later versions. Ultimately, in their fast battleships, the British opted for 15in (38cm) guns – a size of gun which the Germans only matched when the Bayern class entered service, with its own 38cm guns. Another initial problem was the wasteful turret layout in dreadnoughts of the Nassau class, where no attempt was made to provide across-deck arcs of fire. The subsequent Helgoland class represented an improvement, though, as did the introduction of superfiring mounts in the Königs and Bayerns. The Bayerns, with their centreline-mounted 38cm guns, represented the ultimate wartime development of German naval ordnance.

The use of smaller-calibre ordnance did not necessarily equate to markedly shorter range or effectiveness. The 28cm SK L/45 or L/50 gun mounted in the earlier German battlecruisers and the Nassaus had a muzzle velocity of 855–880m/sec (2,805–2,887ft/sec), which equalled the performance of their British counterparts' 12in gun. The weapon also had a maximum effective range of 18,100m (19,790yds), which was improved by 1,000m after Dogger Bank, thanks to mounting modifications which increased the guns' muzzle elevation to 16 degrees. The 30.5cm SK L/50

The development of the Bayern class of dreadnoughts represented a major step forward for the *Kaiserliche Marine*. Arguably these were the best capital ships of the war, with a combination of good speed, excellent protection and a powerful main battery of eight 38cm (15in) guns. This photograph shows the forward turrets of *Bayern*, which became the fleet flagship after entering service two months after Jutland.

gun had a poorer performance (850m/sec and 16,200m), but again during 1915 the range increased to 20,400m thanks to improved elevation. This, though, was partly compensated for by the heavier weight of armour-piercing shell; 405kg for the 30.5cm shell compared to 300kg for the 28cm one.

What really set the German guns apart from the British ones was the fire control systems they used. The finest of guns were useless unless their shells were capable of consistently hitting their target; accuracy depended on rangefinding, and correcting the fall of shot. Both relied on optical rangefinders or telescopes, which in turn supplied the information that was fed to a plotting system inside the ship's citadel. These tracked the relative position, course and speed of firing ship and target ship, and then mechanically calculated a firing solution. This was passed to the turrets, allowing the ship to fire an accurate and coordinated salvo. Spotters then observed the fall of shot, and fed this information back into the system to improve the accuracy of the ship's gunnery.

Initially, the *Kaiserliche Marine* adopted a fire control system known as *Standgerät* (St.G), which did not rely on the mechanical plotters being introduced into the Royal Navy. Tirpitz himself thought it unlikely that gunnery would

GERMAN GUNNERY SUPERIORITY: THE CLASH OF BATTLECRUISERS AT JUTLAND, 31 MAY 1916

After initial sparring the battle of Jutland began in earnest when the two battlecruiser forces met. Vizeadmiral Hipper had already turned towards Vizeadmiral Scheer's battle fleet, which was approaching from the south-east. Hipper hoped he could lure Beatty's ships into an ambush. The two lines of battlecruisers – five Germans and six British – were on parallel courses, with the British nine miles to the west of the Germans. Hipper's ships opened fire first at 1548hrs, and then the British replied. From the start, however, it was clear that the Germans were firing more accurately, although both sides scored hits: within 12 minutes *Lion*, *Tiger* and *Seydlitz* all had one of their turrets knocked out. By 1600hrs the range had dropped to seven miles. Then, at 1602, *Von der Tann* struck *Indefatigable* with two salvos in quick succession, and the British battlecruiser blew up.

By then the four fast battleships of Rear Admiral Evan-Thomas's 5th Battle Squadron had joined the fight, and they began firing on the rearmost German ships. Meanwhile, Hipper and Beatty continued on to the south, exchanging salvos as they went. Other ships were hit, including *Moltke*, *Von der Tann* and *Seydlitz*. At 1621, *Queen Mary* was struck by a shell from *Derfflinger*. This started an internal fire, and four minutes later a huge explosion ripped the battlecruiser in two. This prompted Beatty to utter his famous line to his flag captain: 'There seems to be something wrong with our bloody ships today!'

At 1648hrs, the light cruiser *Southampton*, scouting ahead of Beatty, spotted the German battle fleet approaching from the south-east. Beatty immediately ordered his ships to turn about, and so avoid the trap. They managed it, thanks to the covering fire of the fast battleships, and a distracting melee between British destroyers and German torpedo boats which screened Beatty's withdrawal. Scheer had come within minutes of trapping Beatty, thanks to Hipper's skill in enticing his opponent southwards. During that hour of fighting, German gunnery had proved to be highly effective – and deadly. Their salvos landed with greater accuracy, thanks to a faster and more efficient targeting system and better rangefinders. This more than compensated for the larger calibre of the British guns. Above all though, it was poor safety procedures on board the British battlecruisers that consigned over 2,000 men to their deaths in *Indefatigable* and *Queen Mary*.

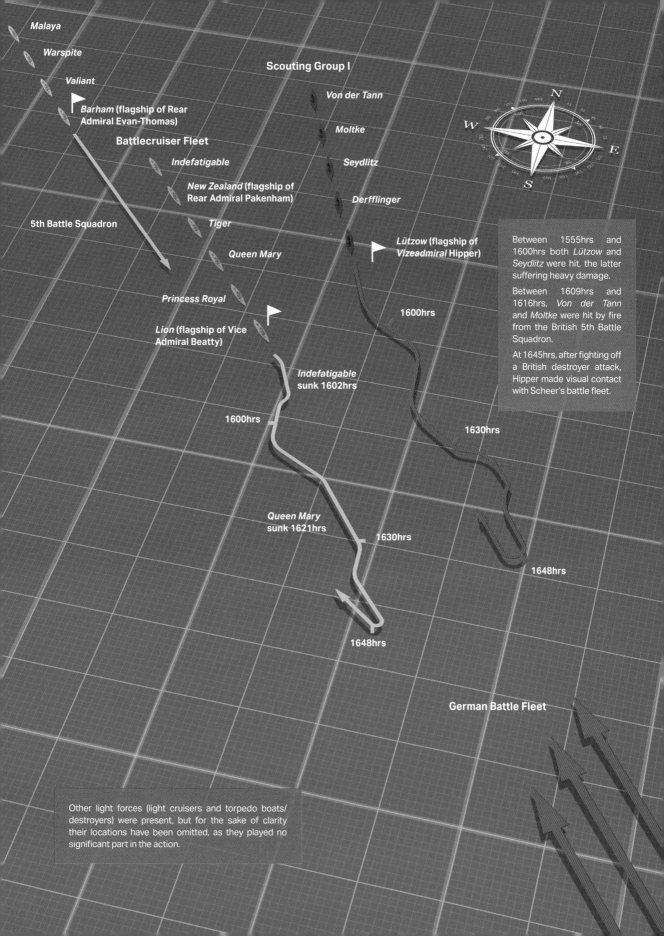

Malaya

Warspite

Valiant

Barham (flagship of Rear
Admiral Evan-Thomas)

Battlecruiser Fleet

Indefatigable

New Zealand (flagship of
Rear Admiral Pakenham)

5th Battle Squadron

Tiger

Queen Mary

Princess Royal

Lion (flagship of Vice
Admiral Beatty)

Scouting Group I

Von der Tann

Moltke

Seydlitz

Derfflinger

Lützow (flagship of
Vizeadmiral Hipper)

1600hrs

Indefatigable
sunk 1602hrs

1600hrs

Queen Mary
sunk 1621hrs

1630hrs

1648hrs

1630hrs

1648hrs

German Battle Fleet

Between 1555hrs and
1600hrs both *Lützow* and
Seydlitz were hit, the latter
suffering heavy damage.

Between 1609hrs and
1616hrs, *Von der Tann*
and *Moltke* were hit by fire
from the British 5th Battle
Squadron.

At 1645hrs, after fighting off
a British destroyer attack,
Hipper made visual contact
with Scheer's battle fleet.

Other light forces (light cruisers and torpedo boats/
destroyers) were present, but for the sake of clarity
their locations have been omitted, as they played no
significant part in the action.

be conducted at ranges over 6,000m, and so it was 1908 before a German equivalent to the British Dumaresq system[3] was adopted. The clumsily named *EU/SV-Anzeiger* trigonometrical computation system and range-rate clocks was less comprehensive than its British equivalent, and it placed a greater reliance on both the artillery officer's judgement, and on the efficiency of the *Richtungsweiser* (Direction) rangefinders and spotters. Fortunately the Germans had the best optical equipment of the period. In 1908, Zeiss stereoscopic rangefinders were introduced, which simplified rangefinding.

The main difference between the two systems was that the German one produced firing solutions more rapidly than its British counterpart. Gunnery was controlled by the artillery officer from the conning tower, where he stood next to the captain, to ensure an easy flow of information between the two, and had his own team, complete with periscope. The system worked well at Dogger Bank and Jutland, when German gunnery was found to be accurate at both medium and long range, despite the often-trying visibility conditions imposed by funnel smoke. Another factor was the flight of the shells themselves. The Germans had a less efficient means of converging fire from all of a ship's turrets, so that the shells all landed on the same spot. Nevertheless, the shells themselves flew more accurately thanks to a more efficient burn rate of their propellant charge when they were still in their barrels.

Propulsion

The capital ships of the High Seas Fleet began at a disadvantage compared to the British, thanks to Tirpitz's rejection of turbine engines as a means of capital ship propulsion, and their continued reliance on coal. In all German pre-dreadnought battleships, and in the Nassau and Helgoland classes of dreadnought, triple-expansion reciprocating engines were used, despite the greater size and weight of these systems, and their lesser efficiency. Prototype turbines had been built in Germany but were not yet considered reliable enough to use. However, by 1908 all new German cruisers and destroyers were fitted with turbine engines, and by 1911 British-designed Parsons turbines were being built in Germany under licence for use in the third class of dreadnoughts, and in the latest battlecruisers.

The first German capital ship to be fitted with turbines was *Von der Tann*. The battlecruiser was powered by Parsons-Marine AEG engines, with high-pressure versions serving the two outer shafts, and low-pressure ones driving the inner shafts. Each was fed by steam from several Schutz-Thornycroft small-tube boilers, also built under licence. These were purely coal-fired, but from 1916 on these were augmented by sprayed tar-oil. This effectively set the pattern for all subsequent German capital ships, although in the Derfflingers and

---

3   The Dumaresq system was a mechanical calculating device, first developed in 1902 by Lt John Dumaresq RN. Effectively it was an analogue computer which, in combination with rangefinding devices, dramatically improved the effectiveness of naval gunnery when it was introduced into service before World War I.

The SMS *Von der Tann* was the first of the High Seas Fleet's battlecruisers. Unlike the battlecruiser's British counterparts, the balance between speed, firepower and armour was less skewed; with the main battery being of smaller calibre than early British battlecruisers. Turbine-powered, *Von der Tann* was both faster and better protected.

the *Hindenburg*, and in the Kaiser, König and Bayern classes of dreadnought, supplemental oil-fired systems were also provided.

One disadvantage of German capital ships compared to their British counterparts was speed. This was largely the result of the greater German emphasis on protection, which increased the weight of the ship being pushed through the water. It was also influenced by other things, including the inferiority of the brown lignite coal available to Germany, which burned less efficiently than the anthracite used in British ships. Also, German engines, despite often being copies of British ones, tended to produce a lower power output, which in turn meant a slower speed. This speed advantage allowed the British battlecruisers (commanded by Vice Admiral David Beatty) to overhaul their German counterparts at Dogger Bank, and let them evade the pursuing German battle fleet at Jutland. In general these differences were fairly minimal, compared to the advantage enjoyed by the Germans in terms of protection.

LIGHT FORCES

The Germans viewed their light forces differently from the British. In addition to their combined main roles of fleet reconnaissance and trade protection, a third role also developed, as light cruisers were used as command vessels for destroyer flotillas. During the war a fourth function, minelaying, was also added, with most German light cruisers being adapted for the purpose. Two Brummer-class minelaying cruisers were also laid down during the war, and these entered service in 1916.

Development was fairly constant, from the ten-ship Gazelle class of 1895 to the wartime Köln class, two of which entered service in early 1918. Until the advent of the Pillau class in 1914–15, all of these were armed with 10.5cm (4.1in) guns, which lacked the firepower of most modern British cruisers of the period. However, the 15cm (5.9in) guns of later German cruisers gave them parity with their Grand Fleet counterparts. This increase in armament was matched by a continual increase in both speed and displacement. From 1904 steam turbine propulsion was used, and speed increased steadily from 21½ knots in the Gazelles to 27½ knots in the later cruisers, despite a doubling of displacement.

Most German light cruisers carried torpedoes, either 45cm (17.7in), 50cm (19.7in) or 60cm (23.6in) ones. Of these, the first were mounted in submerged tubes, and were of minimal offensive value, but from the Pillau class on these were usually deck mounted, making them much more practical. Nevertheless, they were still not especially useful, as they lacked accurate targeting devices, and they were never carried in sufficient quantities to produce an effective spread of torpedoes. Instead, it was Germany's large fleet of torpedo boats (or destroyers) that were the primary torpedo-armed warships of the High Seas Fleet. While gunnery was the main arbiter of victory in a naval battle, the Germans also placed a significant emphasis on the use of torpedoes, and therefore a great deal of care and attention was given to the use of torpedo boats within the fleet.

Boats tended to be designed and built in half flotillas of five boats, and each group incorporated changes from the previous batch. As a result, while their basic design remained approximately the same, incremental changes resulted in a gradual improvement in the quality and performance of these vessels. Turbine engines were used exclusively from 1908 on, although during the war several older reciprocating-engine torpedo boats remained in service. In general terms, though, while German torpedo boats were smaller than the destroyers used by the British, they represented a far more cost-efficient design, while remaining an equally potent offensive threat.

As in the cruisers, torpedo sizes mounted in torpedo boats increased over the years, with 50cm torpedoes being introduced in 1911. Most boats carried six tubes, in single or twin mounts. The G6 torpedo carried a 164kg warhead, and had a range of up to 8,400m at 27 knots. German tactics called for a mass torpedo launch by one or more flotillas to maximize the chances of hitting a target, but in the end, when this was tried at Jutland, no hits were achieved.

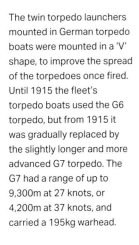

The twin torpedo launchers mounted in German torpedo boats were mounted in a 'V' shape, to improve the spread of the torpedoes once fired. Until 1915 the fleet's torpedo boats used the G6 torpedo, but from 1915 it was gradually replaced by the slightly longer and more advanced G7 torpedo. The G7 had a range of up to 9,300m at 27 knots, or 4,200m at 37 knots, and carried a 195kg warhead.

HOW THE FLEET OPERATED

ORGANIZATION

In August 1914 the High Seas Fleet was a large and well-balanced entity, with what the German Naval Command considered was the right mix of warships to carry out its somewhat vague primary mission. With a few exceptions, the dreadnoughts and pre-dreadnoughts of the battle fleet were grouped into divisions according to class:

I Division	Helgoland-class dreadnoughts
II Division	Nassau-class dreadnoughts
III Division	Deutschland- and Braunschweig-class pre-dreadnought battleships
IV Division	Deutschland-class pre-dreadnought battleships
V Division	Kaiser-class dreadnoughts

When the König class of four dreadnoughts fully entered service in early 1915, these made up the V Division. At the same time the Kaiser-class dreadnoughts were redesignated as the VI Division. There were only minor changes to the composition of these battle squadrons during the course of the war. The most significant of these was the formation of Battle Squadron IV in December 1916, following the commissioning of the first of two new Bayern-class dreadnoughts.

The fleet's complement of battlecruisers and cruisers was reduced due to extensive overseas commitments. The battlecruiser *Goeben* and the light cruiser *Breslau* were in the Mediterranean, while the powerful East Asia Squadron consisted of two armoured cruisers and four light cruisers. To make up for this, the 3rd Scouting Group was made fully operational, and added to the fleet during the opening weeks of the war. The 6th Scouting Group (6th SG), a force of nine assorted cruisers (including the modern light cruisers *Magdeburg* and *Augsburg*) was stationed in the Baltic and remained independent of the High Seas Fleet.

The fleet also consisted of eight torpedo boat flotillas (numbered I–VIII), each of which consisted of 11 boats. These were divided into two half-flotillas

FLEET ORGANIZATION

Fleet Flagship (Admiral von Ingenohl) *Friedrich der Grosse*	
Battle Squadron I Vizeadmiral von Lans: 8 dreadnoughts	
I Division (von Lans)	*Ostfriesland* (flag), *Thüringen, Helgoland, Oldenburg*
II Division (Konteradmiral Gaedecke)	*Posen* (flag), *Rheinland, Nassau, Westfalen*
Battle Squadron II Vizeadmiral Scheer: 8 pre-dreadnought battleships	
III Division (Scheer)	*Preussen* (flag), *Schlesien, Hessen, Lothringen*
IV Division (Kommodore Mauve)	*Hannover* (flag), *Schleswig-Holstein, Pommern, Deutschland*
Battle Squadron III Konteradmiral Funke: 4 dreadnoughts	
V Division (Funke)	*Prinzregent Luitpold* (flag), *Kaiser, Kaiserin, König Albert*
Scouting Forces (Konteradmiral Hipper)	
1st Scouting Group (Hipper): 3 battlecruisers, 1 armoured cruiser	*Seydlitz* (flag), *Moltke, Von der Tann* (flag, Konteradmiral Tapken), *Blücher*
2nd Scouting Group (Konteradmiral Maas): 7 light cruisers	*Köln* (flag), *Mainz, Stralsund, Kolberg, Rostock, Strassburg, Graudenz*
The Reserve Squadrons	
Squadron IV Vizeadmiral Schmidt: 7 pre-dreadnought battleships, deactivated in November 1915	*Wittelsbach* (flag), *Wettin, Mecklenburg, Schwaben, Braunschweig* (flag, Konteradmiral Alberts), *Elsass, Zähringen*
Squadron V Vizeadmiral Grapow: 7 pre-dreadnought battleships, deactivated in November 1915	*Kaiser Wilhelm II* (flag), *Wilhelm der Grosse, Kaiser Barbarossa, Kaiser Friedrich III* (flag, Commodor Begas), *Kaiser Karl der Grosse, Brandenburg, Wörth*
Squadron VI Konteradmiral Eckermann: 8 coastal defence battleships, deactivated in August 1915	*Hildebrand* (flag), *Heimdall, Hagen, Frithjof, Ägir* (flag, Konteradmiral Behring), *Odin, Beowulf, Siegfried*
3rd Scouting Group No commander assigned: 5 light cruisers	*Munchen, Danzig, Stuttgart, Frauenlob, Hela*
4th Scouting Group Konteradmiral von Reubers-Pashwitz: 4 armoured cruisers	*Roon* (flag), *Yorck, Prinz Adalbert, Prinz Heinrich*
5th Scouting Group Konteradmiral Jasper: 4 protected cruisers, deactivated in September 1914	*Hansa* (flag), *Vineta, Victoria Louise, Hertha*

of five boats apiece, and were commanded by the 11th boat, the flotilla leader. On the outbreak of war all the flotillas were amalgamated into the fleet, having previously been independent of the High Seas Fleet command structure. The final flotilla, Torpedo Boat Flotilla VIII, was also only formed in August 1914.

The core of the fleet consisted of the fleet flagship and three battle squadrons. Supporting the battle fleet were the battlecruisers and cruisers of the Scouting Forces, grouped under one command. There was also a Reserve Fleet made up of older pre-dreadnought and coastal defence battleships which were mobilized at the start of the war. However, these were never deployed on operational duties with the fleet. In early 1915, when the König-class dreadnoughts joined the fleet (becoming Division IV of Battle Squadron III), the Braunschweig-class pre-dreadnoughts *Preussen* and *Lothringen* were transferred into the Reserve Fleet, joining Squadron IV.

COMMAND AND CONTROL

In theory the High Seas Fleet was its own independent entity, albeit one that formed the major part of the *Kaiserliche Marine*. Its mission had been established, and its considerable resources allocated to it, and organized into subordinate commands. In theory too, its commander-in-chief, one of the most experienced naval officers in Germany, had the freedom to plan and carry out its wartime operations. In practice, however, throughout the war, while its own command structure remained largely unchanged, he and his fleet were subjected to controlling forces from other, higher quarters. As a result, for most of the war the fleet commanders had very little leeway to conduct naval operations on their own initiative. Instead, they were constrained by often-contradictory instructions and rules of engagement. Operational doctrine too could also be influenced by these external constraints, not least of which was the whim of the German Emperor.

Naval Command

In the Imperial Germany of 1914, Kaiser Wilhelm II was both the country's head of state and the head of its armed forces. This meant he was the commander-in-chief of the *Kaiserliche Marine*. While this was also technically true of King George V and the Royal Navy, the British monarch was merely the fleet's titular head, with no operational authority. By contrast the Kaiser was very much the supreme commander of the navy, with the authority vested in him to exert his control as he pleased. The Kaiser controlled military, naval and civil affairs by means of a series of cabinets. In the German army, though, the Kaiser's authority was limited, as he commanded it through the medium of his General Staff. Similarly in civil matters, the civil government ran the country in his name, through the German parliament. With the *Kaiserliche Marine*, though, there was no intermediary body.

Effectively the navy's higher levels of command existed to carry out the Kaiser's orders. Even *Grossadmiral* von Tirpitz, as Secretary of State of the *Reichsmarineamt* (Imperial Naval Office) was there to advise and guide the Kaiser, rather than to control the fleet in his titular name. On his accession to power the Kaiser disbanded the *Kaiserliche Admiralität* (Imperial Admiralty), and split its functions into three smaller bodies. The *Reichsmarineamt* was effectively a Naval Ministry, similar to the British Admiralty or the US Navy Department, albeit a body concerned primarily with naval budgets, administration and shipbuilding. A second body, the *Marinekabinett* (Naval Cabinet) dealt with stores, munitions and the governance of naval officers, including promotions, pay and appointments. Most of the time the Kaiser allowed these two bodies to function without excessive interference.

Admiral von Tirpitz resigned his post as Secretary of State in September 1916, at which point Admiral Eduard von Capelle was appointed in his stead. Two years later, when the Kaiser sought a more aggressive head of the Navy Office, von Capelle was asked to resign. By that stage of the war the *Kaiserliche Marine* was in turmoil, and two successors, Admiral Paul Behnke, who had commanded a battle squadron at Jutland, and then Admiral Ernst Ritter von Mann briefly held the post during the final weeks of the war. The *Marinekabinett* was ably run

Although the commander-in-chief of all Imperial German forces, Kaiser Wilhelm II had a particularly proprietorial interest in the navy, and so dictated the strategic and operational missions given to the High Seas Fleet. (From the oil painting by Claus Bergen, (1884–1965), *The Kaiser Addressing the High Seas Fleet After the Skagerrak Battle)*

by Admiral Georg von Müller throughout the war, until the same chaotic period at its end. Until then, however, the *Kaiserliche Marine* was administered with notable efficiency. A final administrative office was that of the Inspector-General of the Navy, a post that was held throughout the war by the Kaiser's brother, Prince Henry of Prussia.

All operational matters of the *Kaiserliche Marine* were the preserve of the *Kaiserliches Oberkommando der Marine* (Naval High Command). This was the body that directly controlled the actions of the High Seas Fleet. At the start of the war its chief was Admiral Hugo von Pohl, but when the Kaiser ordered him to take command of the High Seas Fleet his place was taken by *Vizeadmiral* Gustav Bachmann. He in turn was replaced seven months later by Admiral Henning von Holtzendorff. Like Tirpitz, Bachmann had disagreed with the Kaiser over unrestricted U-boat warfare, and paid the price. Von Holtzendorff held the post until August 1918, at which point he was replaced by Admiral Reinhard Scheer. By then, though, the post had changed, and so Scheer became the chief of the grandly named Supreme Naval High Command, which was based at the Kaiser's war headquarters in Spa.

The *Oberkommando der Marine* was a purely advisory body, designed to support the Kaiser in naval matters. Its chief was assisted by his *Admiralstab* (Admiralty Staff) whose real function was to serve as a link between their ultimate commander-in-chief – the Kaiser – and the commander of the active battle fleet – the High Seas Fleet. However, the *Oberkommando* maintained a naval intelligence section and an operational planning department, which was effectively there to support the High Seas Fleet, and to a lesser extent naval forces in the Baltic theatre, and on detached service overseas. This structure, though cumbersome, achieved two things. It provided the commander of the High Seas Fleet with the expertise he needed in the preparation of fleet operations, and it served as a conduit between the fleet commander and his ultimate superior, Kaiser Wilhelm.

The real problem was the Kaiser himself. Unlike the naval officers who served him, he lacked a thorough grounding in naval matters, and was more likely to act impulsively or be influenced by his own personal viewpoint than his professional subordinates. He was also unused to the concentrated workload that his naval responsibilities demanded. The army high command had largely managed to exclude the Kaiser from its operations, but the Kaiser had a more proprietorial relationship with the navy, and could not be so easily excluded. He often referred to the High Seas Fleet's warships as 'his ships', and was protective of the fleet to the extent of being risk-averse. This led to the Kaiser's orders that caused the wartime fleet to make the safeguarding of the fleet the primary consideration in any sortie. As a result, the High Seas Fleet would operate under an immense and stifling handicap.

Fleet Command

Officially, the High Seas Fleet was the name given to the battle fleet of the *Kaiserliche Marine*. The name was first used on 16 February 1907, when the 'Home Battle Fleet' was renamed. It too had been the result of a rebranding five years earlier, when the existing seasonal battle fleet was formed into a permanent active force. However, the High Seas Fleet was officially based in Wilhelmshaven, while Kiel became the base for the navy's Baltic Command. It therefore never incorporated these Baltic squadrons, or those serving overseas, such as the East Asia Squadron. In August 1914 the High Seas Fleet was commanded by Admiral Friedrich von Ingenohl, who flew his flag in the modern dreadnought *Friedrich der Grosse*. The Commander-in-Chief of the High Seas Fleet also had a headquarters ashore in Wilhelmshaven.

The Admiral was served by a small naval staff, controlled by his chief of staff. In August 1914 this post was held by a captain (*Kapitän* Ernst Ritter von Mann Edler von Tiechler), but by 1 September the post became the preserve of *Vizeadmiral* Richard Eckermann. Other chiefs of staff would follow, with *Kapitän* Michaelis holding the post throughout 1915, and *Konteradmiral* Adolf von Trotha from January 1916 until the end of the war. His primary job was to act as the trusted adviser of the fleet commander – his right-hand man. His other duties included ensuring that the Fleet Staff worked efficiently and that any problems arising within the fleet were dealt with.

The Fleet Staff included sections responsible for fleet administration, signals, maintenance and repair, manning, logistics, pay, medical provision, charts and navigation, training and intelligence-gathering, while other smaller departments dealt with more specific matters, including ordnance, torpedoes, fleet and base liaison, meteorology, educational development and religion. Other major semi-autonomous sections dealt with U-boats and naval aviation, and operational planning, although the latter answered directly to the *Oberkommando der Marine*. To confuse matters further, many of the administrative, repair and weapons-related sections were officially provided by the North Sea Naval Station, who provided the fleet's shore facilities, and played 'host' to it.

At sea, though, the fleet's commander-in-chief embarked a much smaller staff, which naturally included his own chief of staff, and a number of officers – primarily those concerned with purely operational matters, such as planning, intelligence, navigation, weapons, signals and medicine. The Admiral himself was expected to concentrate on his operational duties while at sea, with all other staff officers there to support him, and to provide their admiral with specialist knowledge in their particular field. The difference of course between command afloat and ashore was communications. Once at sea the flagship could maintain wireless contact with the shore, and so with the commander-in-chief's superiors in the Naval High Command, but in practice such ship-to-shore signals were limited to instructions to the North Sea Station to prepare for fleet arrivals, or repairs.

Once at sea the fleet's commander-in-chief had to coordinate the actions of his various squadrons, and to react speedily to any intelligence he received. The capital ships of the battle fleet generally operated together, and so for the most part were within visual signalling range of each other. However, for most of the war, the commanders-in-chief tended to rely on wireless signals to issue their orders. This obviously left their communications open to interception by the enemy. Each battle squadron of the battle fleet had its own squadron commander – a highly experienced officer of flag rank – while the squadron itself was divided into two divisions, with the second division commanded by his subordinate, another more junior flag officer.

The battle fleet was usually under the direct command of the commander-in-chief, and at Jutland consisted of three battle squadrons of dreadnoughts and pre-dreadnought battleships, a scouting group of light cruisers and three destroyer flotillas. While the battle squadrons and the scouting group had their own commanders, the torpedo boats were commanded through a torpedo boat force commander, in this case a commodore, who flew his broad pennant in a light cruiser. He then in turn passed on his orders to the various flotilla leaders. The fleet's attached U-boat arm was officially part of the High Seas Fleet, as was the Naval Air Service. The U-boats had no direct radio contact with the fleet, and so all signals from them were passed on to the fleet from the U-boat flotilla headquarters on shore in Wilhelmshaven, Helgoland or Emden. The same was true of the Zeppelins of the Naval Air Service, although they could usually contact fleet warships nearby using short-range wireless.

The dreadnoughts of the High Seas Fleet's battle fleet, photographed while at sea from a Zeppelin. This was the line-astern formation Scheer deployed the fleet into during the opening stages of the battle of Jutland, when the spacing was half the 1,000m 'bridge to bridge' distance shown here.

As the Scouting Forces of the High Seas Fleet usually operated independently of the battle fleet, it had a similar but smaller staff structure when at sea. *Vizeadmiral* Hipper, commander of the Scouting Forces, was accompanied on his flagship (*Seydlitz* or *Lützow*) by a chief of staff and by a small group of staff officers. Hipper assumed direct command of the battlecruisers of the 1st Scouting Group, and on occasion a second-in-command was appointed to assist him, flying his own flag in another battlecruiser. His real deputy, though, tended to be the flag officer commanding the 2nd Scouting Group, which was made up of light cruisers. At Jutland Hipper commanded the 1st Scouting Group, while *Konteradmiral* Bödicker commanded the 2nd, flying his flag in the *Frankfurt*. Three torpedo boat flotillas were also attached to Hipper's force, which he commanded through *Kommodore* Heinrich in the light cruiser *Regensburg*.

Fleet Control

By August 1914 the High Seas Fleet had become a highly trained force, thanks to frequent exercises and fleet manoeuvres. In fact, in most cases there was little leeway for tactical finesse. The dreadnoughts of the High Seas Fleet, as well as the pre-dreadnought battleships and the battlecruisers, were designed to engage the enemy with their full broadsides. This meant that like the ships-of-the-line of the Age of Sail, these German capital ships, in the same way as their British counterparts, had to deploy in line of battle. This created problems in terms of command and control. After all, with the entire German battle fleet in line astern, the column of ships at Jutland extended for almost six nautical miles (nm).

Each of the 16 dreadnoughts and six pre-dreadnought battleships in the line were normally spaced 500m apart – roughly 2½ cables, or a quarter of a nautical mile. This, however, was measured from bridge to bridge, or rather from the bridge of one ship to the foremast of the ship in front. A junior officer or midshipman would be responsible for accurate station keeping using a small hand-held ranging device, and calling for small modifications in the ship's speed to maintain the correct position. With a capital ship measuring some

The High Seas Fleet on manoeuvres shortly before the outbreak of war. Here, pre-dreadnought battleships of the Wittelsbach class, as well as an attached light cruiser – presumably the torpedo boat leader – have been interpenetrated by a line of torpedo boats after a dummy torpedo run. Training, of course, was two-sided – the officers commanding the battle fleet had to know how to react to the threat posed by a mass torpedo attack.

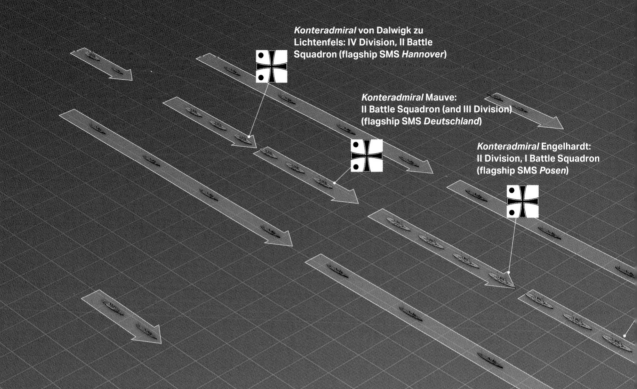

Konteradmiral von Dalwigk zu Lichtenfels: IV Division, II Battle Squadron (flagship SMS *Hannover*)

Konteradmiral Mauve: II Battle Squadron (and III Division) (flagship SMS *Deutschland*)

Konteradmiral Engelhardt: II Division, I Battle Squadron (flagship SMS *Posen*)

THE IMPERIAL GERMAN BATTLE FLEET AT SEA

This shows the deployment of the main body of the High Seas Fleet during the sortie that led to the battle of Jutland. The capital ships of the battle fleet were arrayed in line astern, with the two squadrons of dreadnoughts leading, and the squadron of pre-dreadnoughts following astern of them. These three battle squadrons were flanked by the torpedo boat flotillas and light cruisers attached to the battle fleet, and more torpedo boats and light cruisers were ranged ahead and astern of the main body. The aim was that if the enemy was encountered, the battle fleet was already deployed in its battle array, and merely needed to turn to present its main guns to the enemy force.

Of course, it was unfortunate for *Vizeadmiral* Scheer that at Jutland the enemy battle fleet was not sighted before it appeared ahead of this column of warships, and at right angles to it. This meant that Scheer's 'T' had been crossed, as the guns of the British dreadnoughts could concentrate their fire on the head of the German column. If the circumstances had been different, and German Scouting Forces had located the main body of

the British Grand Fleet beforehand, then Scheer would have had advance warning of the trap. He could then have turned his battle fleet, so that it was not placed at a disadvantage during the gunnery duel that would follow.

In order to maintain this cruising formation, the bridge crew of each warship had to be acutely aware of their position within the fleet, and in maintaining the correct distance between them and other ships. This of course meant near-constant adjustments in speed and heading. Scheer's own flagship was placed near the centre of the line of dreadnoughts, which was considered the optimal position from which to control the battle. Conversely though, when this formation was ambushed by the British at Jutland, Scheer was positioned too far astern to have a clear view of the situation, as the British threat was partly obscured by haze and funnel smoke. His actions though, once the danger was appreciated, proved decisive. Scheer was able to turn this whole formation about and reverse its course, thereby avoiding the British trap.

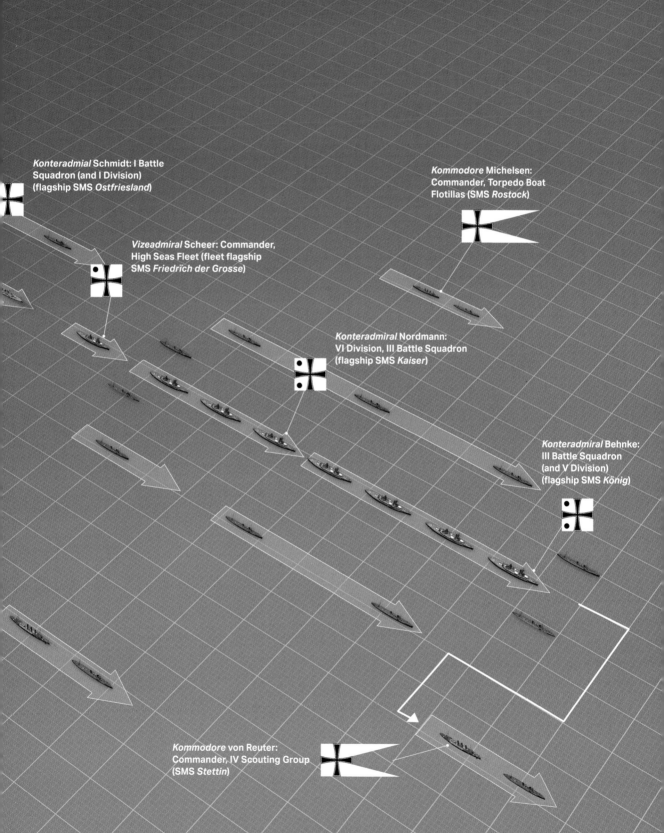

Konteradmial Schmidt: I Battle Squadron (and I Division) (flagship SMS *Ostfriesland*)

Kommodore Michelsen: Commander, Torpedo Boat Flotillas (SMS *Rostock*)

Vizeadmiral Scheer: Commander, High Seas Fleet (fleet flagship SMS *Friedrich der Grosse*)

Konteradmiral Nordmann: VI Division, III Battle Squadron (flagship SMS *Kaiser*)

Konteradmiral Behnke: III Battle Squadron (and V Division) (flagship SMS *König*)

Kommodore von Reuter: Commander, IV Scouting Group (SMS *Stettin*)

128–180m long, this reduced the distance between ships to around 300m. Hence, if the ship ahead was hit and suddenly lost power, at 20 knots the dreadnought astern would collide with the casualty in just over 30 seconds. Therefore captains had to be ready to take evasive action with little warning. For this reason, unless closed up tight for a gunnery action, the German battle fleet usually operated at 1,000m intervals.

Manoeuvring this column usually involved turning in succession, following the lead ship. In effect, the leading ship would turn onto the new course, then the rest of the fleet would continue on their original course until they reached the leading ship's turning place, and then they too would turn to follow. This was a fairly straightforward manoeuvre, but as happened at Jutland, it also meant that an enemy fleet could target the turning point, and so pound each ship in the fleet on reaching that same spot. That was why the Germans introduced their *Gefechtskehrtwendung* ('Battle Turn-Away') manoeuvre, when the whole line of ships turned at the same moment, before settling on a reciprocal course in the opposite direction. This was a risky manoeuvre, as it greatly increased the risk of collision, but the High Seas Fleet practised it regularly, and at Jutland this training paid off.

As a line of 22 capital ships was unwieldy, another option was to steam in parallel columns made up of squadrons of 6–8 ships, or divisions of 3–4 vessels. This had the advantage that signalling any change of course was more straightforward, as the ships were usually in sight of their neighbouring column, usually 1,000 or 2,000m on their beam, depending on circumstances. These columns could also be turned into line, with the end column forming the lead in a line-astern formation, and the other columns turning to take up station astern of this lead ship. This, again, required practice to get it right. Fortunately

The battlecruiser SMS *Lützow*, flagship of the Scouting Forces, was so badly damaged at the battle of Jutland and experienced flooding so extensive that it was impossible to make it back into port. Vizeadmiral Hipper was forced to transfer his flag, while Kapitän Harder and his crew continued the battle to save their ship. (From the oil painting by Claus Bergen, *Hipper Leaving Lützow for SMS Moltke*)

for the High Seas Fleet, it had a large and secure practice ground behind the defensive minefields which stretched from Helgoland to Horns Reef off the Danish coast. Therefore exercises in ship handling and station keeping were commonplace, until the national shortage of coal limited the ability of the fleet to put to sea from early 1917 on.

Other formations were also used. The battle fleet could turn through 90 degrees so each ship was abeam of the next one, or it could form up in echelon, with each ship following a bearing. These, though, were unusual evolutions, as it was hard to re-form the battle line afterwards. Also, during the Dogger Bank battle in January 1915, *Konteradmiral* Hipper deployed his four battlecruisers in echelon, so each ship was slightly astern and abeam of the next in line. This allowed him to use the aft-firing guns on his battlecruisers to return the British fire, while still heading away from them at full speed, yet allowing him to switch into an angled line of battle if required.

For the most part the fleet's battle squadrons operated as a single entity during their sorties, as did the clustered torpedo boat flotillas, who had their own evolutions, based around their ability to launch massed torpedo attacks. In their case the boats tended to operate in half-flotilla columns of 5–6 boats, either in line abreast or in echelon, turning simultaneously to launch their torpedoes. The Scouting Forces, though, while having the option to manoeuvre in the same way as the battle fleet, were usually dispersed, in order to perform their primary role of searching out the enemy. In this case the 1st Scouting Group of battlecruisers would act as a rallying point for the cruisers, who would be strung out in line far ahead of them, but within visible distance of each other. The aim, of course, was to cover the largest possible area of sea in their search.

The fleet flagship SMS *Friedrich der Grosse* firing the main battery of 30.5cm (12in) guns. This picture was supposedly taken during the battle of Jutland from the bridge of the SMS *Ostfriesland*, flagship of Battle Squadron I. By that time the battle line had been closed up, so there was just 300m between the stern of one dreadnought in the line and the bow of the next.

Communicating the wishes of an admiral was a difficult business at sea. At night signal lamps could be used, and in daylight flag hoists or semaphore flags could be used. However, given the often-poor visibility prevalent in the North Sea, the High Seas Fleet tended to make extensive use of wireless, regardless of the security risk this posed if their signals were intercepted by the enemy. To take the opening hours of Jutland as an example, one of Hipper's light cruisers, the *Elbing*, used wireless to report the sighting of an enemy cruiser at 1527hrs. Hipper used flag hoists to turn

his battlecruisers towards the enemy ship, and used another flag hoist to set their new speed. Three minutes later *Konteradmiral* Bödicker in the *Frankfurt* ordered his light cruisers to close with the flagship, to give him the firepower he needed if they encountered the enemy.

Over the next hour both Hipper and Bödicker exchanged sighting information with each other, and Hipper passed the key ones on to Scheer in the fleet flagship, out of sight to the south. However, once both Scouting Groups had closed up, their commanders used visual signals to order changes of course, speed or target. This exchange continued for the best part of an hour before the initial clash between scouting forces evolved into the duel between Hipper and Beatty's battlecruisers known as the 'Run to the South'. Incidentally, when Scheer learned of the sighting of Beatty's force, he ordered his battle fleet to close up from 1,000m to 700m between ships. He would reduce this to 500m later that evening, just before he encountered the dreadnoughts of the Grand Fleet, under the command of Admiral John Jellicoe.

COMMUNICATIONS AND INTELLIGENCE

In modern parlance, the three cornerstones of successful military organizations and operations are command, control and communications. Although the command-and-control elements have already been discussed, efficient communications were vital to both. In addition, effective naval operations relied on the ability to acquire and evaluate information on the enemy, and to disseminate this within the fleet command structure. That way the fleet commander and his subordinates knew roughly what to expect during a sortie, and they were able to take steps to deploy and fight the fleet accordingly. Therefore, in terms of the High Seas Fleet, communications and intelligence-gathering were vital to its success.

Communications

Until the 1880s communications between warships at sea had been carried out in the time-honoured way it had always been – by the exchange of visual signals. Flag hoists had been used in the Age of Sail, and were still a useful means of naval communication. These had their limitations, however, as poor visibility or even the angle of the flag due to the wind could affect the ability to transmit messages. The Royal Navy pioneered the use of signal lamps during the late 1860s, and although they initially used their own coding system, this soon evolved into signal communications using Samuel Morse's system. By 1914 the *Kaiserliche Marine* had adopted its own *Blinkgerät* (flashing device) system of optical Morse transmitters. These had a theoretical range of 8,000m at night, and half that in daylight.

Although the *Blinkgerät* lamps were more reliable than flag hoists, in the High Seas Fleet both tended to be used when transmitting visual signals – flags in port, or when in close formation, and *Blinkgerät* when at sea. A limitation, though, was the ability of the enemy to see visual signals at night, and even if they could not be read, the flashing would give away the signalling ship's position. This happened during Jutland, when both sides spotted enemy signal lamps operating at night, and reacted accordingly. The other problem was the rate of *Blinkgerät* transmission – around 12 to 14 words per minute. As a result, at Jutland, the signal 'Alter course, leading ships of divisions together, the rest in succession, 2 points to starboard' sent by Scheer to the rest of his battle fleet using *Blinkgerät* at 1829hrs that evening, would have taken roughly a minute to transmit, and a little longer for the receiving yeomen in the receiving ships' bridge crews to pass on the message to their captains.

However, this was less important than the limited range. A visual signal like the one above would also be repeated by the divisional flagships down the long line of the battle fleet, which would have further added to transmission time. Consequently, in most cases these were linked to a preparative flag hoist. After the signal was sent and acknowledged, the fleet commander would order the manoeuvre to be executed. At that moment the preparatory flag would be lowered, and the same flag signal repeated by the watchful yeomen on the divisional flagships. Therefore, the execution of the manoeuvre would be virtually instantaneous.

The obvious limitations of visual signalling meant that when at sea, and to communicate with Wilhelmshaven, the commanders of the High Seas Fleet tended to rely on wireless communications. In Germany the radio revolution had begun in 1887 when the physicist Heinrich Hertz first demonstrated a new short-wave radio device, which used Morse telegraphy. By 1907, when the High Seas Fleet was created, a more effective version of the same Hertz system was in the process of being adopted by the *Kaiserliche Marine*. Within two years every German warship had its own wireless transmission (W/T) offices fitted with a Telefunken vacuum tube wireless set. Typically, in most capital ships, three W/T offices were built, to reduce the risk of communications being knocked out in battle.

The battlecruiser SMS *Seydlitz* served as the flagship of the fleet's Scouting Forces until the eve of Jutland. It was from here that *Vizeadmiral* Hipper not only commanded the fleet's Scouting Forces, but also Zeppelins and aircraft used for fleet reconnaissance.

As a member of Scouting Group I, the battlecruiser SMS *Moltke* was well-equipped with powerful wireless equipment which allowed her commander to communicate not just with other battlecruisers in the group, but also other forces in the area including Zeppelins and the fleet commander.

The tactical radio range for these tube sets was still fairly short – under 20–30nm in most ships, or just over the horizon, and even this was dependent on favourable atmospheric conditions. Larger, high-powered long-range systems were used for ship-to-shore communications, but most ships lacked the equipment to generate high-frequency signals. These were fitted to fleet and squadron flagships, and of course in a string of shore-based radio stations located on the German coastline, or its islands. These had the range to transmit signals anywhere in the North Sea basin.

The adoption of wireless created its own difficulties. First, the signalling ship, if it was out of sight of the recipient, would have to transmit its own position as well as the message. This increased the risk of poor navigation or mis-tapped

The open bridge of a König-class dreadnought gave its commander, in this instance *Kapitän* Seiferling, an excellent view in all directions apart from astern. On the bridge wing a yeoman stands ready to give semaphore flag signals while signal flags are flying from the starboard side of the foremast. (From the oil painting by Claus Bergen, *Bridge of SMS Markgraf*)

coordinates leading to a misleading report. Messages, when encrypted, had to be encoded, sent to the W/T room, and then sent. Then in the receiving ship the same process had to be done in reverse. All this took time, and delays of up to 30 minutes were not uncommon. Typically, though, a message would be sent within six minutes of drafting, and read in plain text by the recipient within 12–15 minutes of first being penned. At times, however, these delays could be crucial.

The proliferation of W/T use also created another problem. There was now a potential for the enemy to intercept signals, so instead of transmitting them in plain Morse, a codebook, the *Signalbuch der Kaiserlichen Marine* (SKM), was used for the majority of all German naval W/T signals. However, it was captured by the Russians in late August 1914, when the cruiser *Magdeburg* ran aground in the Baltic. The British were given a copy, and so were able to break the German signal codes. Although these changed periodically, the Admiralty cryptographers were usually able to decipher the new version. It was not until May 1917 that a completely new system was created which the Allies were unable to decipher.

Intelligence

The gathering of intelligence on enemy fleet movements was of crucial importance during the war, and the High Seas Fleet maintained its own naval intelligence section. By 1914 a number of wireless signal stations had been built around the coast, often linked to Zeppelin fields. These were used to monitor British naval signals, and as early as November 1914 they had some success intercepting and deciphering some of these. It was late 1915 before the *Kaiserliche Marine* set up its own *Entzifferungsdienst* (Deciphering Service), but its performance was lacklustre, and little of real note emerged from it. Crucially, virtually none of these deciphered naval signals had anything to do with the Grand Fleet. The department did monitor the volume of British naval signals, to serve as an indicator of when the Grand Fleet put to sea, but generally the British were better served in this field.

One of the problems was that the Germans were unaware that the SKM codes had been broken until later in the war. They also used W/T extensively, while the British tended to maintain radio silence while at sea, if at all possible. While the Germans could gather some direction-finding information from intercepted German signals, the British could too, and the greater volume of German traffic made this a more effective form of intelligence-gathering for them than it did for the Germans. All this was rarely enough. The British failed to detect the German sortie in November 1914, while the Germans never knew the Grand Fleet was at sea before Dogger Bank or Jutland. Therefore, signals intelligence was an indicator, not a singularly reliable source of information. Instead, the High Seas Fleet tended to rely on more conventional sources – U-boats, airships and its own Scouting Forces.

The *Kaiserliche Marine* built the first of its *Unterseeboote* (or 'U-boats') in 1906, and by August 1914 it had 28 of them in service, compared to the Royal Navy's 55 submarines. The U-boat fleet was greatly expanded during the war, and the capabilities of these craft improved steadily. Although some advocated using these to unleash an unrestricted war against British merchant shipping, there was no clear plan for their use. A number were used as minelayers around the British coast, and a number of boats on active patrol enjoyed success against British warships. However, until the restrictions on attacking merchantmen were gradually removed – the first in 1915, then more in 1916, and finally all lifted in 1917 – there was no major emphasis on the sinking of Allied merchantmen. Therefore, this created an opportunity for the High Seas Fleet.

Admiral von Ingenohl quickly realized the potential of U-boats as intelligence-gatherers, and flotillas were thus attached to the fleet. Primarily, this meant lying off the Grand Fleet's principal base in Scapa Flow, as well as the secondary ones in the Cromarty Firth and the Firth of Forth, to report by wireless on any fleet sailings. This mission was of limited effectiveness. Visibility range from a surfaced U-boat was restricted, particularly at night or in bad weather. Before Jutland, *Vizeadmiral* Scheer had deployed a similar screen of U-boats, and these failed to warn him that the Grand Fleet and the Battlecruiser Fleet had both sailed.

In theory, airships provided a more effective means of intelligence-gathering. In 1911 an experimental naval air station was established, and a Zeppelin-building programme began the following year. The first of these airships, *L-1*, entered service later that year. A series of accidents, however, meant that when the war began only one airship, *L-3*, was in service. More would follow, and by the end of the year six Zeppelins were in service. The German Naval Air Service

The Zeppelin *L-30* pictured over the Zeppelin base at Ahlhorn, south of Wilhelmshaven. This served as the headquarters of *Fregattenkapitän* (commander) Strasser, commanding the German Naval Airship Division, where powerful wireless equipment allowed the rapid flow of sighting reports between the headquarters, the Zeppelins and the fleet.

came under the command of *Vizeadmiral* Hipper, commander of the High Seas Fleet's Scouting Forces, which underlined the reconnaissance role of these craft. It also highlighted their shortfall. These Zeppelins were seen as tactical scouts, linked directly to the High Seas Fleet.

Therefore these Zeppelins were never used in a more strategic role, conducting regular and methodical long-range patrols over the North Sea. The Zeppelin force was expanded as more air bases were built, and seaplanes were introduced too. Nevertheless, the strategic limitations of the Naval Air Service remained, and it was never used in a way that would make the most of their range and potential. They were also susceptible to bad weather, and were regularly grounded, especially in winter. Even in better flying conditions, poor visibility over the North Sea frequently limited their effectiveness. Nevertheless, with a maximum visibility range of 60nm (when operating at a height of 4,000m in good weather), these airships still presented the commanders of the High Seas Fleet with a superb intelligence-gathering tool.

During the later stages of the war it became common for Zeppelins to accompany the High Seas Fleet and its Scouting Forces while they were at sea. They could then scout ahead of the fleet, and direct it towards the enemy. It was a powerful reconnaissance tool, and one that the British would attempt to emulate.

When at sea, the High Seas Fleet relied on the most traditional intelligence-gathering tool of all – its own Scouting Forces. Again, with a potential masthead visibility range of 20nm, a light cruiser could be an effective reconnaissance tool. A Scouting Group of several of them, extended into a line within visual sighting range of each other, could cover a much larger area of sea. This was the most reliable intelligence-gathering means at the fleet's disposal, although everything depended on the cruisers looking for the enemy in roughly the right place. Nevertheless, at both Dogger Bank and Jutland it was Hipper's light cruisers that first made contact with the enemy, and allowed both the commanders of the High Seas Fleet and its Scouting Forces to react accordingly.

BASES AND LOGISTICS

Maintaining a naval force the size of the High Seas Fleet was no easy undertaking. Not only did it need a secure, well-defended naval base, but this had to be of sufficient size to accommodate the fleet as it expanded. Not only did the fleet's warships need to be maintained, refitted and repaired, but so did their ordnance

Pre-dreadnought battleships in Wilhelmshaven, pictured shortly before the outbreak of war. While this extensive harbour was well-equipped, the rapid expansion of the navy during the decade preceding the war meant that the port's repair facilities would be overstretched if the fleet suffered damage in a larger-scale fleet action.

and other, often extremely complex, technical equipment. The ships themselves had to be supplied with coal, fuel oil, water, ammunition, naval stores and all of the food and goods needed to supply the needs of the crew.

Wilhelmshaven

In 1853, Prussia struck a deal with the neighbouring Duchy of Oldenburg which saw the transfer to the Prussian crown of a small parcel of land with access to the North Sea at the Jade Bight. A decade and a half later, in 1869,

NAVAL RECONNAISSANCE: THE POST-JUTLAND SORTIE, 18–19 AUGUST 1916

It is one of the fallacies of the naval war that after Jutland the High Seas Fleet never put to sea again. In fact, it made three fleet-sized sorties, in August and October 1916, and again in April 1918. Other operations were planned, but for various reasons they were cancelled at the last minute. In the August sortie, *Vizeadmiral* Scheer made excellent use of both U-boats and Zeppelins to provide him with reports on British naval movements.

In the evening of 18 August 1916, Scheer's High Seas Fleet sortied from Wilhelmshaven, with the intention of drawing elements of the British fleet into battle on favourable terms. Scheer had 18 dreadnoughts and two battlecruisers at his disposal, as well as light cruisers and torpedo boats. His intention was to use *Vizeadmiral* Hipper's Scouting Forces to bombard the port of Sunderland, in an attempt to draw

out Vice Admiral Beatty's Battlecruiser Fleet. Hipper would then draw it onto the massed guns of the German battle fleet, and destroy it before Admiral Jellicoe's Grand Fleet could intervene.

In the end the sortie proved unsuccessful, as thanks to signal intercepts the British reacted faster than Scheer had anticipated. When he learned of this, Scheer abandoned the Sunderland bombardment, keeping Hipper close by him. Then, at 1300hrs on the 19th, word reached him that Commodore Tyrwhitt's Harwich Force was approaching from the south. Scheer decided to attack it instead, but further reports that Jellicoe and Beatty were closing in rapidly with superior forces led to him abandoning the operation and returning to Wilhelmshaven.

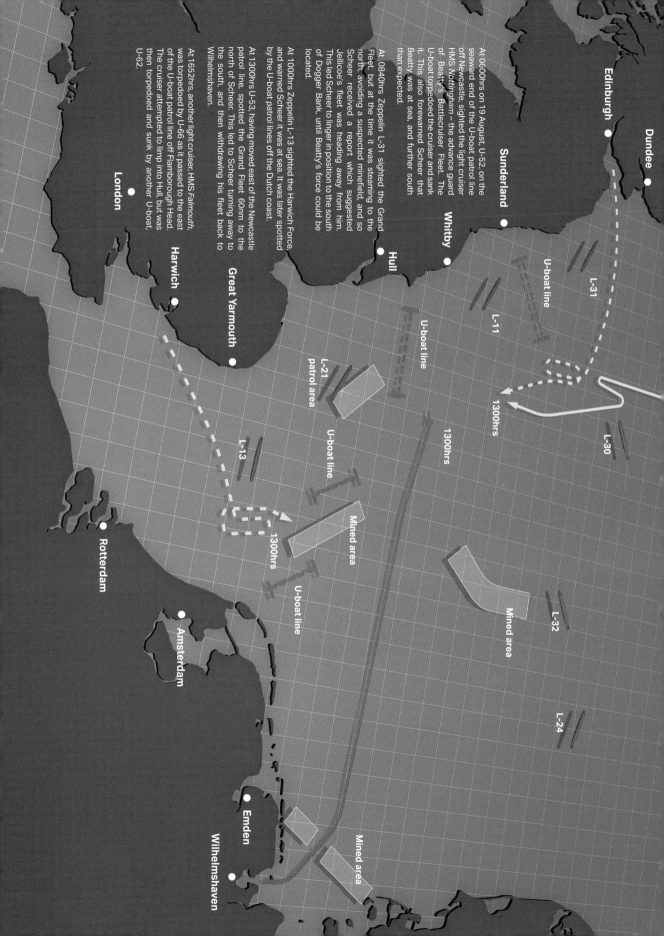

At 0600hrs on 19 August, U-52, on the seaward end of the U-boat patrol line off Newcastle, sighted the light cruiser HMS *Nottingham* – the advance guard of Beatty's Battlecruiser Fleet. The U-boat torpedoed the cruiser and sank it. This also forewarned Scheer that Beatty was at sea, and further south than expected.

At 0840hrs Zeppelin L-31 sighted the Grand Fleet, but at the time it was steaming to the north, avoiding a suspected minefield, and so Scheer received a report which suggested Jellicoe's fleet was heading away from him. This led Scheer to linger in position to the south of Dogger Bank, until Beatty's force could be located.

At 1000hrs Zeppelin L-13 sighted the Harwich Force, and warned Scheer it was at sea. It was later spotted by the U-boat patrol lines off the Dutch coast.

At 1300hrs U-53, having moved east of the Newcastle patrol line, spotted the Grand Fleet 60nm to the north of Scheer. This led to Scheer turning away to the south, and then withdrawing his fleet back to Wilhelmshaven.

At 1652hrs, another light cruiser, HMS *Falmouth*, was torpedoed by U-66 as it passed to the east of the U-boat patrol line off Flamborough Head. The cruiser attempted to limp into Hull, but was then torpedoed and sunk by another U-boat, U-62.

Dundee

Edinburgh

Sunderland

Whitby

Hull

Great Yarmouth

Harwich

London

Rotterdam

Amsterdam

Emden

Wilhelmshaven

U-boat line

L-31

L-11

U-boat line

1300hrs

L-30

1300hrs

L-21 patrol area

U-boat line

L-13

Mined area

Mined area

L-32

L-24

1300hrs

U-boat line

Mined area

Mined area

König Wilhelm I founded a town there, which he named after himself. More importantly, he also started building a naval base there. It included a modest arsenal, depot and repair facilities, but a small shipyard was added too. Two years later, after the end of the Franco-Prussian War, with the elevation of Wilhelm from king to emperor and the unification of Germany, this became the *Kaiserliche Werft Wilhelmshaven* (Wilhelmshaven Imperial Shipyard). The town, the port and the shipyard all expanded dramatically over the years that followed. The shipyard produced its first ironclad warship in 1879, and 20 years later the yard launched its first modern battleship.

By then, Wilhelmshaven had become the home port of the Home Fleet. The port now included several harbours and basins, acres of warehouses and workshops, and no end of coaling sheds, cranes, slipways, tidal locks – everything the fleet might need to function. However, while commodious, Wilhelmshaven had never been designed for such a large fleet, and for ships as large as dreadnoughts. Its real problem was that the port lay on the western bank of the Jade, a large estuary, or more accurately an oval silt-filled bay or bight which was connected to the North Sea by a channel almost 15nm long. The Jade was prone to silting, and so it had to be continually dredged. As it was tidal the harbour itself lay behind lock gates, to limit the ebb and flow.

This in itself posed a problem. The fleet's capital ships drew so much water that they could only enter the Jade around high water. There were also just two main entrances to Wilhelmshaven, plus a third smaller one for the smaller warships and civilian craft. By early 1915 the battle fleet was so large that it took two successive tides, 12 hours apart, for all three squadrons plus the battlecruisers to leave port. In between, half of the battle fleet would anchor in the Jade Reede (Roads) outside the entrances.

Once assembled, it would take the best part of an hour to head northwards through the channel between two mudflats to the open sea, beyond the line of the Ostfriesische Inseln. The large tidal mudbank to the east of the channel lay between the Jade and the river Weser, which in turn led to the neighbouring port of Bremerhaven. At the northern end of the Jade lay Schillig Reede, named after the small town on the western shore. There the fleet would either anchor and await further orders, if it was being held in readiness, or it would form up and set out into the Helgoland Bight of the North Sea.

Wilhelmshaven itself was not particularly loved by the sailors. They called it 'Schlickstadt' (Silt Town), and many found the flat shore and mudflats of that part of the Lower Saxony coast singularly unattractive. Still, as a port designed to support the navy, it had the usual sources of entertainment designed to keep sailors entertained, while for those in need of healthier leisure pursuits there were sports fields and gymnasiums. Some officers actually relished the place, with its golf courses, restaurants, cinemas and 'officer only' wine bars. Many

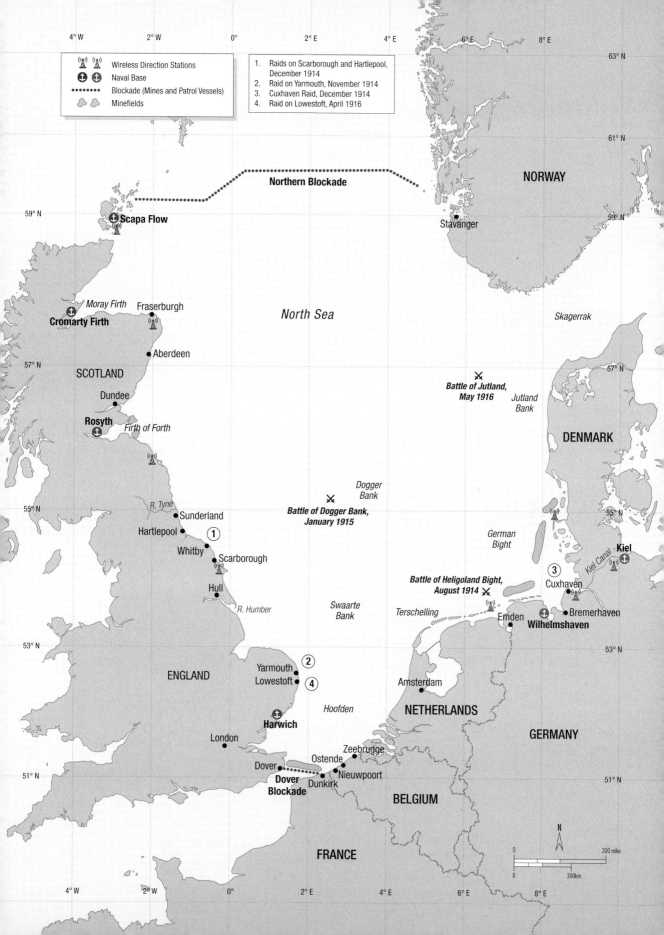

Wireless Direction Stations
Naval Base
Blockade (Mines and Patrol Vessels)
Minefields

1. Raids on Scarborough and Hartlepool, December 1914
2. Raid on Yarmouth, November 1914
3. Cuxhaven Raid, December 1914
4. Raid on Lowestoft, April 1916

4° W   2° W   0°   2° E   4° E   6° E   8° E

63° N

NORWAY

Northern Blockade

61° N

Stavanger

59° N ⊕ **Scapa Flow**   59° N

Moray Firth   Fraserburgh   *Skagerrak*
Cromarty Firth
Aberdeen
57° N   57° N
SCOTLAND   *Jutland Bank*
Dundee   ✗ **Battle of Jutland, May 1916**
Rosyth   *Firth of Forth*   **DENMARK**

North Sea

55° N   *Dogger Bank*   **Kiel**
R. Tyne   Sunderland   ✗ **Battle of Dogger Bank, January 1915**   *German Bight*   55° N
Hartlepool   ①   *Kiel Canal*
Whitby   ③ Cuxhaven
Scarborough   **Battle of Heligoland Bight, August 1914** ✗   Bremerhaven
Hull   *Swaarte Bank*   *Terschelling*   Emden   **Wilhelmshaven**
R. Humber

53° N   53° N
ENGLAND   Yarmouth ②
Lowestoft ④
Amsterdam
NETHERLANDS   **GERMANY**
Hoofden
Harwich
London   Zeebrugge
Ostende
Dover   Nieuwpoort
51° N   **Dover Blockade**   Dunkirk   51° N
BELGIUM

FRANCE

N
0   200 miles
0   200km

4° W   2° W   0°   2° E   4° E   6° E   8° E

officers rented accommodation in Wilhelmshaven, so they could escape from their duties whenever they could. A railway line linked the port to nearby cities such as Bremen, Hamburg and Hannover. In this respect the German sailors were better served than their British counterparts, isolated in Scapa Flow.

In theory, the *Kaiserliche Marine* was divided between two principal naval stations – the Baltic which was based in Kiel, and the North Sea, based in Wilhelmshaven. These had no operational role. Instead, they were primarily support organizations for the Baltic naval command and for the High Seas Fleet. Their remit was to provide dockyard supply and training facilities within their area, as well as to maintain coastal defences. Thus, effectively there were two parallel naval organizations in Wilhelmshaven – one running the port's facilities, and the other the fleet. Both shared headquarters buildings in the town. As a result, extensive communication facilities there ensured the fleet headquarters enjoyed dedicated telephone links to Kiel and Berlin, and to the Kaiser's wartime headquarters, which moved several times during the course of the conflict. These facilities also provided good long-distance wireless links to warships deployed in the North Sea.

Logistics

Wilhelmshaven provided all the shore facilities the High Seas Fleet needed to supply, arm and refuel its warships, and thanks to the *Kaiserliche Werft Wilhelmshaven*, it could also repair them when they were damaged. Warships went through a surprising amount of victualling supplies, from meat, flour, butter, potatoes and beer to cold meats, sausages and tinned goods. The ship's victualling officer was then responsible for apportioning food to the ship's

The battlecruiser SMS *Seydlitz*, pictured alongside her usual berth in Wilhelmshaven near the Kaiser-Wilhelm-Brücke. Supply lighters lie off the port side, while supplies can be seen stacked on the adjacent quayside.

German sailors exercising on the foredeck of a dreadnought. For much of the war, the High Seas Fleet remained in Wilhelmshaven, so keeping the crews fit, trained and motivated was a challenge for the fleet's officers.

galleys. Still, it was never intended that the fleet would remain at sea for more than a few days at a time, so there was no need to supply provisions for extended periods. Given the growing food supply problems in Germany, the men of the High Seas Fleet ate reasonably well. The food was generally cooked in bulk on board, but although plentiful it was of low quality.

Some sailors were even ashamed of the disparity between their own shipboard fare and that of their families. One officer recalled that his family only had swedes and turnips, while on board his cruiser they had meat stews. Even during the 'turnip winter' of 1916–17, a seaman on a cruiser reported: 'We have all we can eat of potatoes, peas, beans and other vegetables, meat, bread and butter.' He was fortunate. By then rations had been cut, and quality had dropped. On the pre-dreadnought battleship *Posen*, by early 1916 meat stews were often replaced by a 'barbed wire entanglement' of tinned meat, dried vegetables and cabbage. Officers, though, enjoyed better fare and larger portions, even as Germany as a whole faced shortage and famine. This inequality was a contributory factor in the naval mutinies of November 1918.

Supplying a warship was as much about providing for the ship and guns as the men. Good rail links allowed both coal and ordnance to be transported from the Ruhr to Wilhelmshaven throughout the war, and a network of narrow-gauge shipyard rail track took these to the quayside next to the ship. Mobile dockyard cranes were also provided to help sway munitions on board, while mechanical conveyer belts were used to reduce the exhausting, backbreaking and filthy labour of coaling ships. A dreadnought consumed several hundred tons of coal a day while at sea, and had a capacity of around 3,000 tons. The

Wilhelmshaven dockyard maintained substantial supplies of coal, and after a sortie all ships were fully replenished.

As the war progressed, coal shortages began to make themselves felt. By late 1916, Scheer was told to be sparing with coal stocks, as there could be no guarantee that the huge quantities required could be supplied. This increasingly limited the ability of the High Seas Fleet to sortie in strength, as sufficient coal reserves needed to be maintained in Wilhelmshaven in case of a direct British threat to the German coast. A similar problem also developed when it came to propulsion systems. In the High Seas Fleet, engines, boilers and other pieces of complex machinery needed to be maintained and occasionally overhauled. As the supply of spare parts became increasingly problematic, warships found themselves unable to remain fully operational.

As early as July 1915, Admiral von Pohl wrote: 'I wanted to make a sortie today, to get the ships moving again, and if possible to attack the enemy. Four ships were reported non-operational for engine defects… it makes one despair that so many ships always require repair, and I am prevented from carrying out my intentions.' Given von Pohl's reluctance to take his fleet to sea his claim of planning a sortie might be questioned, but it certainly highlighted the growing problem. As a result, as the war continued, it became rarer for the fleet's warships to leave port, even for routine fleet manoeuvres and gunnery exercises.

When a sortie resulted in a clash with the enemy, as it did at Dogger Bank (1915) and Jutland (1916), warships might require extensive repairs. *Seydlitz* for example, was hit by three 6in (15cm) shells during the bombardment of Hartlepool in December 1914. On returning to Wilhelmshaven the battlecruiser went into the *Kaiserliche Werft*, and spent five days being repaired. The following

During the battle of Jutland, the battlecruiser SMS *Derfflinger* was hit 31 times and suffered extensive flooding damage. In this case a 13.5in shell hit the German dreadnought on the port side of the forward superstructure, almost immediately below the bridge.

month, in January 1915, *Seydlitz* was badly damaged during the Dogger Bank action when the after turrets were knocked out. This time the extensive repairs took over two months, but were completed by 1 April. Just over three weeks later, on 24 April, *Seydlitz* struck a mine 40 miles to the west of Helgoland, which damaged the starboard-side submerged torpedo compartment and caused extensive flooding. The following day the ship entered the floating dock of the *Kaiserliche Werft*, and this time repairs lasted for four days.

Just over a year later, on 31 May 1916, *Seydlitz* was extensively damaged during the battle of Jutland, sustaining 23 large-calibre hits and shipping over 2,000 tons of water. The battlecruiser was lucky to make it home to Wilhelmshaven, as the flooding continued as *Seydlitz* limped home. Once there, lying too low in the water to pass through the locks into the dockyard, the battlecruiser was forced to anchor in the Jade Reede. Instead, while divers sealed the holes below the waterline, the crew lightened the ship, which then managed to pass through the gates to reach the *Kaiserliche Werft*'s now-familiar floating dock on 13 June – two weeks after the battle. This time *Seydlitz* remained in the floating dock until 30 July, at which point the battlecruiser was taken alongside the shipyard quay, where repairs continued until 2 October.

Seydlitz was only one of several warships in the fleet to be damaged at Jutland. Sixteen of its dreadnoughts and five battlecruisers took part in the battle. Another dreadnought, the *König Albert*, was in refit in the shipyard at the time. The battlecruiser *Lützow* was lost, and four of the remaining battlecruisers and seven dreadnoughts were damaged, some including *Seydlitz* needing extensive repairs. Dockyard workers swarmed over the ships in an effort to render the fleet battleworthy again. Nevertheless, a month after the battle only *Rheinland*, *Helgoland* and *Westfalen* had re-joined the battle fleet. All had suffered relatively light damage. It was the end of July before *Ostfriesland*, *König*, *Grosser Kurfürst* and *Markgraf* returned to service, bringing the two dreadnought squadrons back up to full strength. The battlecruisers would remain in dry dock until August, when *Moltke* and *Von der Tann* were repaired, but *Seydlitz* and *Derfflinger* only joined them in October. The repair of damaged light cruisers and destroyers was a lesser priority, and many of them would remain out of action until the end of the year.

This highlighted another problem facing the High Seas Fleet. While the repair facilities in the *Kaiserliche Werft Wilhelmshaven* were excellent, the shipyard only had a finite repair capacity. Towing damaged capital ships through the Kaiser Wilhelm Canal to Kiel was extremely problematic, so the damaged ships remained in Wilhelmshaven. By contrast the Grand Fleet had a choice of first-class shipyards and dockyards to use, and so by sharing the repairs between several yards they could be completed more speedily. After Jutland, despite the best efforts of the *Kaiserliche Werft*, the High Seas Fleet's *Kräfteausgleich* stratagem had become numerically impossible. As a result, for the most part, the fleet remained in Wilhelmshaven, and it was left to the navy's U-boat arm to continue the fight.

COMBAT AND ANALYSIS

THE FLEET IN COMBAT

The High Seas Fleet may have been built as an extravagance, and the strategic role it had been assigned – of breaking British naval superiority – was essentially a self-sacrificing one. However, when war came, the fleet's Commander-in-Chief Admiral Friedrich von Ingenohl was reluctant to expend this immensely powerful force without a better reason than some vague Mahanian precept which offered no guaranteed reward. Better, then, to husband the High Seas Fleet and use it more defensively. In fact, he was convinced that the British would launch an immediate attack. When this did not take place, von Ingenohl contemplated a range of offensive operations, all designed to lure the British out, and then to pounce upon an isolated part of the Grand Fleet. What he conspicuously avoided, despite prompting from the commander of his Scouting Forces, was any attempt to break the British distant blockade.

The Opening Months

In fact, the British had been busy, establishing their blockade and protecting the British Expeditionary Force as it was shipped to France. Then, early on

When the war began the Kolberg-class light cruiser SMS *Köln* was the flagship of *Konteradmiral* Maas' Scouting Group, which was based in Wilhelmshaven. On 28 August 1914 Maas led them into action at the battle of Helgoland Bight. His cruisers, though, were ambushed by British battlecruisers; *Köln* was crippled and Maas was killed. The surviving crew scuttled the ship.

28 August, they struck. Essentially the battle of Helgoland Bight (1914) involved a raid against the German coastal defences near the island of Helgoland, 33 miles from the High Seas Fleet's base at Wilhelmshaven. A gap had been left in Germany's defensive minefield there to allow sorties, and this was guarded by destroyers. When British light forces appeared and drove back the destroyer screen, the supporting cruisers *Stettin* and *Frauenlob* were sent to help. More light cruisers were ordered to sea to join them, but while engaging their British counterparts in a confusing melee, a squadron of British battlecruisers appeared. These tipped the battle, which ended with the loss of three German light cruisers, *Mainz*, *Köln* and *Ariadne*.

The battle was over before the German battlecruisers put to sea from Wilhelmshaven, their delay caused by their need to raise steam. Their appearance two hours earlier might have saved the day for the *Kaiserliche Marine*. This could have been avoided if the Germans had been forewarned of the attack. Consequently, the mine defences were expanded, the destroyers retained for use with the battle fleet, and pre-dreadnoughts and anti-submarine vessels were employed to bolster defences within the protective belt of minefields. The battle also led to the deployment of U-boats in the North Sea to provide early warning of enemy sorties, and regular Zeppelin sweeps along the likely avenues an enemy sortie might take.

However, Helgoland did not really test the High Seas Fleet as an entity – only the effectiveness of German naval defences. Von Ingenohl remained convinced of the need to lure the enemy to sea, where small elements could be ambushed and destroyed, but the Kaiser was risk-averse and refused to allow an operation that might lead to a fleet action at unfavourable odds. Small raids, though, would be countenanced, therefore *Konteradmiral* Hipper planned a sortie on 3 December, which saw the German Scouting Forces venture across the North Sea to Great Yarmouth in an attempt to test the stratagem. The port was bombarded, but only light local forces were encountered, as a lack of warning of the German sortie had left Beatty insufficient time to intervene. Therefore, while the operation might have achieved little, it did suggest that further raids of this kind were feasible.

In mid-December Hipper tried again. The Naval High Command still insisted that the battle fleet be held in reserve, so once again only the Scouting Forces were available. It sailed on 15 December, with the mission of bombarding the British coastal towns of Hartlepool and Scarborough and laying mines off the enemy coast. The battlecruisers of the 1st Scouting Group were accompanied by the 2nd Scouting Group's light cruisers and destroyers. Naval intercepts forewarned the British, and

The battlecruiser SMS *Von der Tann*, photographed while bombarding Great Yarmouth at around 0820hrs on the morning of 3 November 1914. In line ahead are Hipper's flagship *Seydlitz* followed by *Moltke*, and then *Blücher*, largely obscured by *Von der Tann*'s foredeck.

Beatty's battlecruiser fleet was sent south to intercept Hipper. Once again they were too late. *Derfflinger* and *Von der Tann* successfully bombarded Scarborough and then Whitby, while to the north *Seydlitz*, *Moltke* and the armoured cruiser *Blücher* did the same to Hartlepool. The whole bombardment lasted just over 40 minutes before Hipper's ships disappeared back into the mist.

This time, however, von Ingenohl was taking no chances and brought out the battle fleet, sailing as far west as Dogger Bank. Their job was to escort the Scouting Forces home if it was attacked. This was a smart move, as Beatty's force did its best to intercept the raiders. Of course, von Ingenohl anticipated this, but his hoped-for ambush of Beatty using the battle fleet was stymied by poor visibility and rough seas. In fact, apart from slight damage to *Blücher* and *Moltke* from shore batteries, the whole operation went off without a hitch. While this boosted morale within the High Seas Fleet, it caused consternation in Britain. Some 92 people had been killed in the bombardments, and hundreds more injured – most of them civilians. Afterwards, though, von Ingenohl was chided by the Kaiser for his caution, despite obeying Wilhelm's risk-averse orders.

The British, however, were about to have their revenge. On Christmas Day they used three seaplane carriers and seven aircraft to launch a raid on the German Zeppelin base at Cuxhaven. The launch point was to the north-west of Helgoland, outside the German minefield belt. The Cuxhaven raid proved unsuccessful as the Zeppelin base was undamaged, and four of the aircraft

LURING OUT THE BRITISH: THE BOMBARDMENT OF HARTLEPOOL, SCARBOROUGH AND WHITBY, DECEMBER 1914

This limited sortie gives a good idea of how the High Seas Fleet operated before Jutland. *Konteradmiral* Hipper's Scouting Groups left Wilhelmshaven at 0400hrs on 15 December. The bombardment force consisted of the battlecruisers *Seydlitz* (flagship), *Moltke*, *Von der Tann* and *Derfflinger*, the armoured cruiser *Blücher* and the minelaying light cruiser *Kolberg*. Hipper made a dog-legged approach to the English coast to avoid the fishing grounds of the Dogger Bank. Before dawn on 16 December he divided his forces. The escorting light cruisers and destroyers returned home, while the rest divided into two groups.

To the north, *Seydlitz*, *Moltke* and *Blücher* bombarded Hartlepool from 0926 to 0942hrs, firing 1,150 shells, which caused 93 casualties, all but seven of whom were civilians. In return the three warships were slightly damaged by coastal batteries and local destroyers. Meanwhile, the southern group of *Von der Tann*, *Derfflinger* and *Kolberg* headed for Scarborough, and the battlecruisers bombarded the port from 0903 to 0923hrs. Leaving *Kolberg* to sow mines, the battlecruisers headed north to bombard Whitby (1006–1013hrs) before retiring out to sea.

Meanwhile, Admiral von Ingenohl's battle fleet had sortied from Wilhelmshaven and lingered off Dogger Bank, ready to escort Hipper home. The Grand Fleet learned of the sortie, but while the battle fleet never reached the area, Beatty's battlecruiser force almost made contact with the German battle fleet, but turned north and, apart from a clash between a destroyer and a German cruiser, no contact was made. By 0900hrs on 19 December the High Seas Fleet was safely back in the Jade. This type of operation, with Hipper's Scouting Forces being protected at a distance by the battle fleet, would be repeated again.

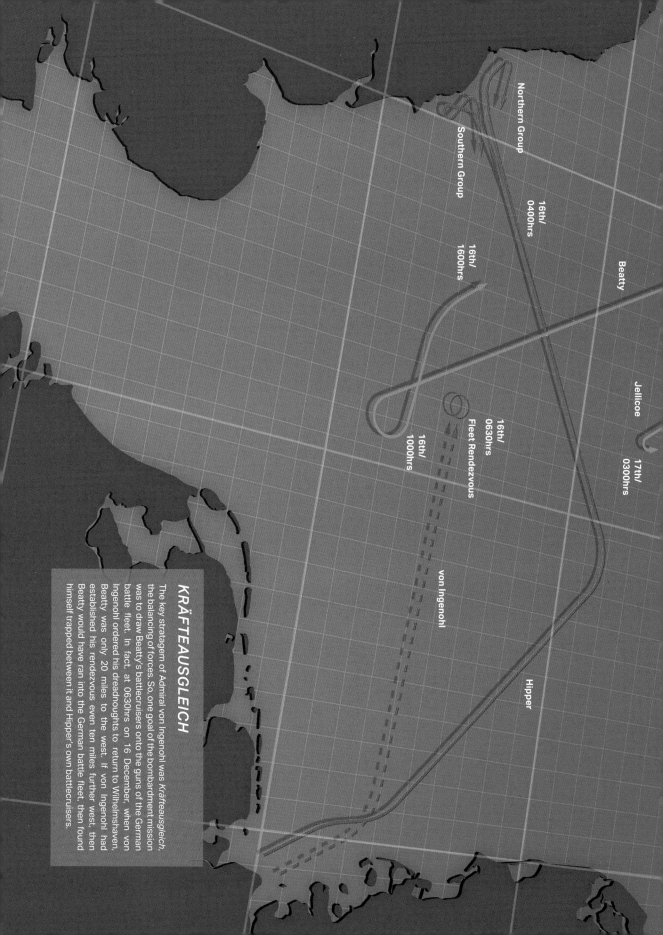

Northern Group

16th/
0400hrs

Southern Group

Beatty

Jellicoe

17th/
0300hrs

16th/
1600hrs

16th/
0630hrs

Fleet Rendezvous

16th/
1000hrs

von Ingenohl

Hipper

KRÄFTEAUSGLEICH

The key stratagem of Admiral von Ingenohl was *Kräfteausgleich*, the balancing of forces. So, one goal of the bombardment mission was to draw Beatty's battlecruisers onto the guns of the German battle fleet. In fact, at 0630hrs on 16 December, when von Ingenohl ordered his dreadnoughts to return to Wilhelmshaven, Beatty was only 20 miles to the west. If von Ingenohl had established his rendezvous even ten miles further west, then Beatty would have ran into the German battle fleet, then found himself trapped between it and Hipper's own battlecruisers.

were forced to ditch. Still, it represented a milestone in naval aviation. It also highlighted the British preoccupation with 'the airship menace', even though the Cuxhaven Zeppelins were primarily used for naval reconnaissance. Just as significantly, when the seaplane carrier HMS *Empress* lagged behind the retiring force, it was attacked by Zeppelin *L-6*, and two Friedrichshafen seaplanes of the *Marine-Fliegerabteilung* – a rare and early example of a naval air strike on a moving warship. This attack proved unsuccessful, but marked another first in naval aviation.

Dogger Bank

In the New Year, von Ingenohl and Hipper planned another sweep into the North Sea, drawing on the lessons learned from the previous operation. However, this would be a limited operation designed to catch British 'spy trawlers', stationed around the Dogger Bank, to monitor German radio traffic. They were usually protected by light forces, but as Hipper planned to use his whole Scouting Forces, these could easily be driven off. Therefore, after dark in the late afternoon of 24 January 1915, Hipper's two groups left Wilhelmshaven, and headed towards the Helgoland gap in the minefields. This time, 1st Scouting Group was made up of Hipper's flagship *Seydlitz*, accompanied by *Derfflinger*, *Moltke* and *Blücher*. The armoured cruiser was standing in for the *Von der Tann*, which was in refit. Unfortunately for Hipper, the British learned of the sortie through radio intercepts.

That evening Beatty's battlecruisers put to sea too, sailing from Rosyth, while Jellicoe's battle fleet also left Scapa Flow. The dreadnoughts would remain to the north of Dogger Bank, in case Beatty needed support. But with five battlecruisers, four light cruisers and three destroyer flotillas, Beatty's force was powerful enough. The rival light cruiser screens spotted each other soon after dawn on 25 January. Vizeadmiral Hebbinghaus, commanding 2nd Scouting Group, correctly surmised that the British cruisers were scouting ahead of a more powerful force. Accordingly, he turned away and warned Hipper, who was further to the south. Hipper sensed a trap too and ordered his battlecruisers to turn away and head towards home. He also contacted von Ingenohl in Wilhelmshaven to request support. Therefore, the battle fleet duly put to sea that morning, to escort the Scouting Group home.

As a result, although nobody was fully aware of it, most of the entire High Seas Fleet and Grand Fleet were now at sea. The Dogger Bank sweep now had the potential of turning into the major fleet action both sides were supposedly keen to fight. The trouble was, Beatty's battlecruisers were closer than Hipper thought. Having sighted smoke soon after 0730hrs, Beatty surged ahead with his three more modern battlecruisers, which were three knots faster than their British or German counterparts. The two battlecruiser squadrons were now on a parallel course and, at 0852hrs, Beatty's flagship *Lion* came within range and opened fire. At 20,000 yards, or 10nm, these opening salvos were fired beyond extreme range. He intended that his 'Splendid Cats', the battlecruisers *Lion* and *Tiger* and their sister-ship *Princess Royal*, would engage the leading three German battlecruisers – *Seydlitz*, *Moltke* and *Derfflinger*.

In fact, thanks to a misunderstanding, both *Lion* and *Tiger* fired at Hipper's flagship *Seydlitz*, while initially *Princess Royal* engaged the rearmost German ship *Blücher*. Beatty's two slightly slower battlecruisers *New Zealand* and *Indomitable* were ordered to engage *Blücher* too, when they came within range; the action had evolved into a stern chase, with the British gradually overhauling their German opponents. By now, both groups of battlecruisers had deployed into an echeloned line, so all of the ships could fire at the enemy. Contrary to British claims, the smaller-calibre German guns were also just within range, but Hipper held his fire until the range became less extreme. It was the British, though, who scored the first telling hit, at 0943hrs, when *Seydlitz* was hit by a shell from *Lion*.

It pierced *Seydlitz*'s after turret and exploded in the shell hoist. The resulting fireball travelled down the trunk to the handling room, causing another explosion. Only quick thinking saved the ship, at the cost of more lives. The after magazine was flooded, drowning the men trapped inside. That one 13.5in shell had claimed the lives of 159 men. At that point Hipper radioed von Ingenohl with the message 'Need assistance badly'. The duel continued nevertheless, and at 1001hrs a 28cm (11in) shell from *Moltke* pierced *Lion* below the waterline, inducing a list. Seventeen minutes later Beatty's flagship *Lion* took a real body blow, hit by two 30.5cm (12in) shells from *Derfflinger*.

SCOUTING GROUP I AT DOGGER BANK, 0920HRS, 25 JANUARY 1915 (overleaf)

In late January 1915 the High Seas Fleet sortied in another attempt to lure Vice Admiral Beatty's Battlecruiser Fleet into an ambush. Using *Konteradmiral* Hipper's battlecruisers as bait, the plan was to draw the enemy onto the massed guns of the German dreadnoughts. Instead, thanks to radio intercepts, it was Beatty who ambushed Hipper, early on 24 January. When the two battlecruiser forces intercepted each other, Hipper withdrew towards his own battle fleet. The British battlecruisers had an edge in speed over their German rivals, and gradually began to overhaul them. At 0852hrs Beatty opened fire. At the time his flagship *Lion* was followed by the battlecruisers *Tiger*, *Princess Royal*, *New Zealand* and *Indomitable*. They were ten miles astern of the Germans, on an almost parallel course.

In this running fight Hipper's own flagship *Seydlitz* was followed by the battlecruisers *Moltke* and *Derfflinger*, with the weaker armoured cruiser *Blücher* at the rear of the line. At first the British fire proved ineffectual, and at 0911hrs, once the range had shortened, Hipper gave the order to return fire. This shows the situation at around 0920hrs, when the range had dropped to eight miles. By then the rival forces had adopted an echeloned formation, so that all of their warships could fire on the enemy. In the foreground, Hipper's flagship *Seydlitz* can be seen firing at *Lion*, while in turn receiving fire from both *Lion* and *Tiger*. The slower *Blücher* can be seen falling astern of the faster German battlecruisers. In the fight that followed both *Seydlitz* and *Lion* would be badly damaged, but *Blücher* would be sunk by the combined weight of fire by the British battlecruisers: a sacrifice that gave Hipper the chance to escape with the remainder of his fleet.

The battlecruiser lost power in one boiler room, the electrical systems failed, and the ship was also flooding. *Lion* hauled out of line, and *Tiger* took the lead. The outnumbered Germans were still fighting back hard.

Then, at 1030hrs, *Blücher* was hit by a 13.5in shell from *Princess Royal*, cutting the armoured cruiser's speed to 17 knots, which allowed the two rearmost British battlecruisers to close the range. Beatty ordered them to concentrate on the stricken armoured cruiser, which had now hauled out of the German line. Hipper now faced the decision whether to support *Blücher*, or save his battlecruisers. In fact, given the odds there was no real choice to make. He maintained his course towards the safety of von Ingenohl's fleet. The duel continued, though, with the German gunners having the better of the exchange. At 1041hrs *Lion* was hit again, and like *Seydlitz* this was a turret hit which caused a fire. Beatty's flagship, however, was saved from disaster by the prompt sealing of the magazine and handling room. *Tiger* was hit too, a shell from *Derfflinger* jamming the forward turret and cutting the hydraulic power.

At that crucial point Beatty made a tactical mistake. Believing he was under torpedo attack from a submarine, he altered course, and the ships astern of him did the same. That let Hipper regain the lead, and by the time Beatty had resumed the chase, Hipper had slipped away and all that remained was to sink the stricken *Blücher*. The ship was hit repeatedly, and, with decks ablaze, the armoured cruiser began to sink. Watching and unable to help was the crew of the Zeppelin *L-5*, whose commander recalled: 'The four English battlecruisers fired at her together. She replied for as long as she could, until she was completely

ANATOMY OF AN ENGAGEMENT: DOGGER BANK, 24 JANUARY 1915

Thanks to radio intercepts the British were forewarned of the High Seas Fleet's sortie to the Dogger Bank on 23 January. Admiral Jellicoe took the Grand Fleet to sea from Scapa Flow, but was unable to intercept the enemy. However, Vice Admiral Beatty's battlecruiser force, sailing from the Firth of Forth, was able to overhaul *Konteradmiral* Hipper's Scouting Forces early on 24 January. What followed was essentially a running battle, where the British battlecruisers had a slight edge in speed over the Germans, and so were able to close the range. Still, both sides caused damage to their opponents. On the German side, the armoured cruiser *Blücher* was badly damaged and hauled out of Hipper's line. Hipper's flagship *Seydlitz* was also badly damaged too, having two turrets put out of action. Beatty's flagship *Lion* was badly damaged, while *Tiger* was hit too.

Hipper was saved further loss by Beatty himself. Due to a signalling error, his battlecruisers turned north, with *Tiger* in the lead. This allowed the slower battlecruisers *New Zealand* and *Indefatigable* to catch up, enabling them to concentrate on the crippled *Blücher*, which Hipper had been forced to abandon to fate, to save the rest of his force. Beatty turned away again and due to a misunderstood signal the rest of his battlecruisers followed. Hipper was then able to break contact, aided by a torpedo boat attack and poor visibility. While Hipper was caught by Beatty at Dogger Bank, he managed to extricate all of his ships but *Blücher*, thanks in part to his opponent's errors. The battle caused the Kaiser to change both the High Seas Fleet's commander and its rules of engagement which he now viewed as too risky.

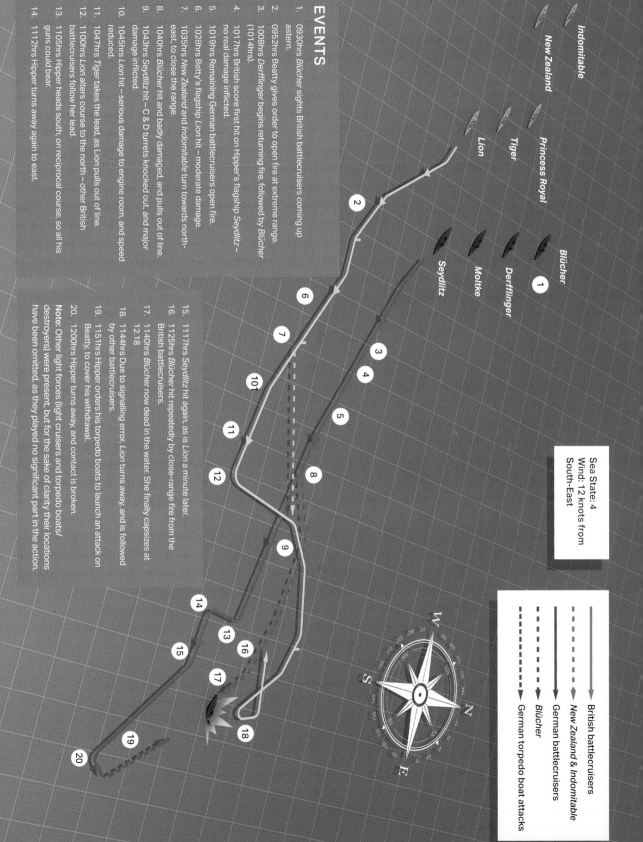

Sea State: 4
Wind: 12 knots from South-East

Indomitable
New Zealand
Princess Royal
Tiger
Lion

Blücher
Derfflinger
Moltke
Seydlitz

EVENTS

1. 0930hrs *Blücher* sights British battlecruisers coming up astern.
2. 0952hrs Beatty gives order to open fire at extreme range.
3. 1008hrs *Derfflinger* begins returning fire, followed by *Blücher* (1014hrs).
4. 1017hrs British score first hit on Hipper's flagship *Seydlitz* – no real damage inflicted.
5. 1019hrs Remaining German battlecruisers open fire.
6. 1028hrs Betty's flagship *Lion* hit – moderate damage.
7. 1035hrs *New Zealand* and *Indomitable* turn towards north-east, to close the range.
8. 1040hrs *Blücher* hit and badly damaged, and pulls out of line.
9. 1043hrs *Seydlitz* hit – C & D turrets knocked out, and major damage inflicted.
10. 1045hrs *Lion* hit – serious damage to engine room, and speed reduced.
11. 1047hrs *Tiger* takes the lead, as *Lion* pulls out of line.
12. 1100hrs *Lion* alters course to the north – other British battlecruisers follow her lead.
13. 1105hrs Hipper heads south, on reciprocal course, so all his guns could bear.
14. 1112hrs Hipper turns away again to east.
15. 1117hrs *Seydlitz* hit again, as is *Lion* a minute later.
16. 1125hrs *Blücher* hit repeatedly by close-range fire from the British battlecruisers.
17. 1140hrs *Blücher* now dead in the water. She finally capsizes at 1218.
18. 1144hrs Due to signalling error, *Lion* turns away and is followed by other battlecruisers.
19. 1151hrs Hipper orders his torpedo boats to launch an attack on Beatty, to cover his withdrawal.
20. 1200hrs Hipper turns away, and contact is broken.

Note: Other light forces (light cruisers and torpedo boats/ destroyers) were present, but for the sake of clarity their locations have been omitted, as they played no significant part in the action.

Legend:
- British battlecruisers
- New Zealand & Indomitable
- German battlecruisers
- Blücher
- German torpedo boat attacks

The armoured cruiser SMS *Blücher* capsizing at the battle of Dogger Bank (24 January 1915) after being disabled by British fire. After Beatty lost contact with Hipper's battlecruisers, his ships rounded on the stricken cruiser, which sank at around noon with the loss of most of the crew.

shrouded in smoke and apparently on fire. At 1207hrs she heeled over and capsized.' Of the 1,200 crew, only 234 lived long enough to be rescued.

Afterwards, both Hipper and von Ingenohl were criticized for their part in the battle. In the case of Hipper this was largely unjustified, as he had done the best he could, given the circumstances. *Blücher* had been his Achilles' heel, but the decision to abandon the armoured cruiser ultimately saved the more valuable *Seydlitz*, which would live to fight another day. Von Ingenohl, though, was rightly censured for not putting to sea earlier to support the Scouting Forces. As *Kapitän* von Egidy of the *Seydlitz* put it: 'If we had known that our main body was behind us, Hipper would not have been forced to abandon the *Blücher*.' Both Tirpitz and Kaiser Wilhelm agreed, and a week later von Ingenohl was replaced. The new Commander-in-Chief of the High Seas Fleet was Admiral Hugo von Pohl, an altogether more cautious commander, who was determined to avoid further losses.

The Long Lull

During the months that followed von Pohl repaired his ships, and instituted changes which would, in theory, spare his dreadnoughts and battlecruisers the catastrophic damage suffered by *Seydlitz*. The High Seas Fleet, however, remained in port for much of 1915, while von Pohl relied on his U-boats to attempt to whittle down the enemy fleet. They achieved little – nothing that would alter the naval balance. Since the war began, four dreadnoughts had been commissioned into the High Seas Fleet, and one battlecruiser. By comparison, by early 1915 the Grand Fleet had been reinforced by five dreadnoughts, a battlecruiser and two new 'fast battleships' – improved dreadnoughts armed with 15in (38cm) guns. This brought the balance of capital ships to a ratio of around 3 to 2, in favour of the British. The British were also outbuilding the Germans, with more 'fast battleships' on the way.

After Dogger Bank, Tirpitz wrote that the battle was a final missed opportunity. He argued that the High Seas Fleet was now too badly outnumbered to have a chance of winning the naval war. This was a message which von Pohl welcomed, as it supported his decision to wage a U-boat campaign. During von Pohl's year-long tenure, however, the naval balance had shifted even more in Jellicoe's favour as those fast battleships entered service.

In January 1916, von Pohl was found to have advanced liver cancer. He was hospitalized and died the following month. On 18 January his place as commander-in-chief was filled by Vizeadmiral Scheer, the former commander of Battle Squadron III. Scheer was well aware of the changing naval balance of power, but he was also sensitive to the growing unease in Germany, as thousands of soldiers died in the trenches, while the High Seas Fleet remained idle in port. He also understood that to meekly cede control of the North Sea to the Grand Fleet was a betrayal of the huge resources Germany had poured into the creation of the battle fleet. By pursuing a more active strategy he hoped to justify the fleet's existence, and to resurrect the policy of *Kräfteausgleich* which von Ingenohl had pursued.

In early March he took the High Seas Fleet to sea and headed south, towards the English Channel. The southern North Sea was empty of British warships, however, and the fleet returned home. He had hoped to lure Beatty south, but the British commander refused to take the bait. This sortie, though, was a much-needed morale-booster for Scheer's men, so another was planned. This time, Scheer resurrected the idea of taunting the British by bombarding coastal ports. Again, the main aim was to lure Beatty to sea. The Scouting Forces sailed from Wilhelmshaven on 24 April, with *Konteradmiral* Bödicker replacing Hipper who was on sick leave. *Seydlitz* struck a mine on leaving the defensive minefields, and had to return to port, so Bödicker shifted his flag into the newly commissioned *Lützow* and continued with the operation.

By dawn the following morning Bödicker's four remaining battlecruisers were off Lowestoft, and spent an hour bombarding the town, before heading six miles north to do the same to Great Yarmouth. Commodore Tyrwhitt's Harwich Force tried to intervene, but they withdrew after a skirmish which saw the cruiser *Conqueror* hit. Of Beatty, though, there was no sign. Scheer's battle fleet was on hand to escort the Scouting Forces home, and for a while he lingered there, hoping Beatty would appear, but by the following afternoon, with fuel running low, he reluctantly returned to port. Both Beatty and Jellicoe had put to sea,

The aftermath of the Dogger Bank action. Here, *Moltke* can be seen astern of the damaged *Seydlitz*, as a Zeppelin flies protectively over the Scouting Group as it limps back to Wilhelmshaven. In the foreground is the knocked-out 'D' turret, where one of its two barrels had lowered into the reloading position just before the British shell struck.

but Jellicoe was too far behind the Germans to intervene, and while Beatty had rashly outstripped the battle fleet, he was also too late to bring the Germans to battle. If he had, then he would probably have proved the value of *Kräfteausgleich*.

Jutland

Jellicoe made another sweep in early May, but to Scheer it also seemed that his counterpart was reluctant to venture further south than Dogger Bank. Therefore, if *Kräfteausgleich* was to happen, Scheer would have to venture further north, into the waters between Dogger Bank and the Skaggerak. For much of May the High Seas Fleet was occupied in the Baltic, but, on 28 May, Scheer gave the orders that would set the next sortie in motion, and would bring about the greatest naval clash of the war. Actually, he issued two sets of orders: one for the Skagerrak option, and the other another bombardment operation, this time at Sunderland. It was only on the afternoon of 30 May that Scheer sent the signal '31 May GG 2490', which notified the fleet that the Skagerrak option had been chosen, and would begin early the following morning. At 0100hrs on 31 May, the Scouting Forces put to sea, with Hipper flying his flag in *Lützow*. The rest of the High Seas Fleet would follow before dawn.

For Scheer, the sortie had two objectives. First, it would give him the chance to harass Allied shipping passing through the Skagerrak, which linked the North Sea to the Baltic. Once there, Hipper's Scouting Forces would conduct the sweep, while the battle fleet remained in reserve to the west of the Jutland peninsula. He also hoped to lure the Grand Fleet to sea, and hoped that, as usual, Beatty would range far ahead of Jellicoe's battle fleet. What he didn't appreciate, though, was that thanks to naval intelligence Jellicoe was already aware of the sortie and was already at sea. The Grand Fleet had left Scapa Flow late on 30 May, while Vice Admiral Jerram's detached squadron of dreadnoughts sailed from the Cromarty Firth. Beatty, now commanding the grandly named Battlecruiser Fleet, followed a more southerly course, heading eastwards from the Firth of Forth. Now all the pieces were in play.

By noon on 31 May Beatty and Hipper were both to the south-west of the Skagerrak and, unknown to each other, were less than a hundred miles apart. If both stuck to their course, contact would be made around 1500hrs, some 65 miles off the Danish coast. At the same time, Scheer was 50 miles south of Hipper, while Jellicoe's battle fleet was 80 miles north of Beatty. This meant that if either battlecruiser force got into trouble, it would take between two and three hours for the respective battle fleets to come to their rescue. Hipper, though, planned that if he encountered Beatty he would run south, to draw his opponent onto Scheer's battle fleet. There was one major difference that day. Jellicoe knew Scheer was at sea, but he had little expectation that the two fleets would make contact. For his part, Scheer had no idea the enemy were at sea, let alone so close.

In fact, first contact was made at 1430hrs, between Hipper's light cruisers and those of Beatty. The battle of Jutland (or the Skaggerak) that followed was the largest naval clash of the war, and in terms of number of ships involved, was the largest naval surface action in history. There is no need to follow its long and complex course here.[4] Instead it is worthwhile examining two segments of the engagement which, taken together, highlight how the High Seas Fleet operated during the battle, and which illustrate the effectiveness of its ships and men.

The battle itself can be divided into several stages. The first was the clash between Beatty and Hipper, which began at 1430hrs and continued until 1730. This saw Hipper's 'run to the south', and the main clash between the battlecruiser fleets that saw Beatty's battlecruisers *Indefatigable* and *Queen Mary* both blow up. Beatty turned away when he sighted Scheer's battle fleet, and the subsequent 'run to the north' saw Beatty attempt the same trick. This was followed by the clash between Jellicoe and Scheer, which lasted until 2030hrs. During this phase the battlecruisers clashed again, and the battlecruiser *Invincible* and the armoured cruiser *Defence* were both blown up. Jellicoe was then thwarted in his plans to ambush the High Seas Fleet thanks to the Germans' deft about-turn.

Contact was resumed, though, further to the west, but Scheer was again able to turn away, this time under cover of an apparent 'death ride' by Hipper's battlecruisers, and a mass torpedo boat attack which forced Jellicoe to break contact. A final brief clash just as darkness fell settled little, and that evening both sides continued on towards the south. Jellicoe hoped to trap the High Seas Fleet, by keeping between it and the northern entrance through the German minefields. Instead, the entire High Seas Fleet managed to find a way past the Grand Fleet by brushing through the light destroyer screen to the stern of Jellicoe's fleet. By dawn Jellicoe's hopes for a renewal of this unfinished battle were thwarted by an empty ocean. That following afternoon the High Seas Fleet safely reached the security of Wilhelmshaven.

Not all of its warships made it home though – both *Lützow* and the pre-dreadnought battleship *Pommern* were lost, as were four light cruisers and five torpedo boats. Yet in terms of losses it was the Grand Fleet that came off the worst. Three modern battlecruisers had blown up, and the British also lost three armoured cruisers and eight destroyers. The death toll of 6,784 British crew and 3,039 Germans also favoured the High Seas Fleet, as did the disparity in tonnage sunk. However, this ignores the strategic and psychological results of the battle, which we will examine later.

Gefechtskehrtwendung ('Battle Turn-Away')

At around 1825hrs on 31 May, Jellicoe's battle fleet had deployed in line ahead, steering towards the west. It was at that moment that they spotted the head of the German battle fleet, also in line ahead, steering north. In naval tactical parlance, that meant that Jellicoe was about to cross Scheer's 'T' – all his broadside guns could fire on the enemy, while only the forward guns of the leading German

---

4   See Charles London, Osprey Campaign 72: *Jutland 1916: Clash of the Dreadnoughts* (2000), or Angus Konstam, *Jutland 1916: Twelve Hours to Win the War*, 2016)

dreadnought could fire back. The leading unit of the High Seas Fleet was *Konteradmiral* Behnke's Battle Squadron III, made up of eight of the fleet's most modern dreadnoughts. The rearmost ship in the squadron was Scheer's flagship, the *Friedrich der Grosse*. Behind this came the eight slightly older dreadnoughts of *Vizeadmiral* Schmidt's Battle Squadron I, and behind them, lagging a bit, were the six pre-dreadnought battleships of *Konteradmiral* Mauve's Battle Squadron II.

In all, some 22 German capital ships were steaming into an ambush made up of the fully arrayed firepower of the British Grand Fleet. Three minutes later, Behnke saw a long ripple of orange flashes through the mist to the north, as the British fleet opened fire. The range was just over 6½ miles. Half a minute later the first salvos began falling around Behnke's flagship and the German dreadnoughts immediately astern of him. The salvos were seen by Scheer too, who immediately realized what was happening. His fleet was trapped. However, the High Seas Fleet had available the only effective means of escape. At 1833hrs he ordered an immediate signal sent to all the ships in the battle fleet. It read 'Turn together 16 points to starboard.' In the German naval manual, this manoeuvre was known as *Gefechtskehrtwendung* ('Battle Turn-Away').

This involved a simultaneous turn, in this case to starboard, by every ship in the battle line. The manoeuvre had been specifically designed to escape exactly the situation Scheer found himself in, and his ships had trained for it during fleet exercises. Now, though, it was being undertaken under fire in the midst of battle. The whole operation depended on initiative and perfect timing. One mistake and the whole manoeuvre could end in collision, disorder and chaos. In the official German history, it all sounded simple: 'The exceptional training of the German fleet … made Scheer feel confident that, in spite of the bend in the line and the enemy's tremendous counter-activity, it would be possible to carry out the intended movement without serious difficulty, even under the heaviest of hostile fire.' At the time, however, there was no guarantee it would work.

To reduce the risk of collision, the last ship in the line would begin its turn first. Once the ship ahead of her saw her turn he would put his own helm over too, and this would be repeated up the line of ships. At Jutland, this was made slightly simpler because the pre-dreadnought squadron had lagged behind the dreadnoughts. This reduced the length of the line to 16 ships. Therefore, on receipt of Scheer's signal to execute the manoeuvre, and on his own initiative, *Kapitän* Redlitch of the *Westfalen* began the turn, and was followed moments later by *Kapitän* Lange of *Posen*. Like the ripple of a Mexican wave the whole manoeuvre worked its way up the line until it reached Behnke in the *König*, which had just been hit by British shells. In the end it all worked perfectly. Each captain knew the limitations of his own ship. For instance, in *Markgraf*, three ships behind Behnke, only two of the three propellers were working and *Kapitän* Seiferling adjusted his speed accordingly.

Within seven minutes the entire German battle line had turned about, and was now steaming out of the trap, and away from the enemy. Afterwards, the German official history claimed that the *Gefechtskehrtwendung* was an emergency measure, and just 'one of the many tactical movements practised for the various eventualities of an action'. This completely understated the significance of the manoeuvre. It was one the Germans had perfected, but it was one the British had not ever considered, let alone practised. Scheer used it as a last resort, and even then it was a manoeuvre that was fraught with danger. Still, it meant that by 1840hrs the thwarted British had completely lost contact with the enemy amid the mist, remnants of smoke screens and thick black funnel smoke that hung over the sea between the two ships. To perplexed British observers, it seemed as if the Germans had simply disappeared into the mist.

Torpedo Attack

After the battle turn-away the two fleets lost contact with each other. However, it also left Scheer's fleet heading towards the south-west, while the British were somewhere to the north-east of him. In order to regain the safety of Wilhelmshaven he needed to head on a more easterly course. Therefore, after extricating his battle fleet he ordered them to turn west-north-west, accompanied by clouds of destroyers and Hipper's battlecruisers. Meanwhile, Jellicoe had turned his battle fleet by divisions, and it was now heading south in a series of parallel columns, each of four dreadnoughts. Shortly after 1905hrs the two groups of dreadnoughts sighted each other, heading on converging

THE 'BATTLE TURN-AWAY' AT JUTLAND, 1820HRS, WEDNESDAY, 31 MAY 1916 (overleaf)

The opening phase of the battle of Jutland involved a clash between the rival battlecruisers, and the detached division of British fast battleships. Inevitably, however, the climax would come when the two rival battle fleets clashed. It was *Vizeadmiral* Scheer's misfortune that when they did meet, he found himself at an immense disadvantage. At the time his battle fleet was in line ahead formation, steering towards the north-east. Then, to the north, the leading German dreadnoughts spotted a line of British dreadnoughts blocking their path. Admiral Jellicoe's battle fleet was steering towards the east-south-east, so effectively he was in a position to 'cross the T' of the German fleet, at a range of just six miles. This meant that all of his dreadnoughts could fire full broadsides at the enemy, while only the forward-facing guns of the leading German dreadnoughts could fire back. It was a potentially catastrophic situation for the German commander.

However, his battle fleet had practised a manoeuvre which was perfect for this appalling situation. The *Gefechtskehrtwendung* (or 'Battle Turn-Away') involved a simultaneous reversal of course by every ship in the German line. At 1818hrs, on his flagship *Friedrich der Grosse*, Scheer sent the signal which set the manoeuvre in train. It read 'Turn together 16 points to starboard'. This shows the manoeuvre under way. The leading German dreadnought *König* attracted most of the British fire, and she was hit several times, as were the other leading ships *Grosser Kurfürst*, *Kronprinz* and *Markgraf*. Still, within five minutes or so the German ships were hidden by smoke, and the British lost contact with them. Scheer had pulled off the seemingly impossible, and saved his battle fleet. Their escape from under the guns of the Grand Fleet was thanks to extensive training, good ship handling and a sizeable slice of luck.

Germany's torpedo boat fleet was designed to operate with the main battle fleet, with the primary purpose of carrying out mass torpedo attacks on enemy capital ships. However, the development of British 'torpedo boat destroyers' designed to counter this threat led to the building of larger German torpedo boats. This one, the *G-101*, was one of four built for the Argentinian Navy, but then incorporated into the *Kaiserliche Marine*.

courses. Effectively, Jellicoe was crossing Scheer's 'T' for the second time in less than an hour. The British opened fire at 1910hrs, by which time the range between the nearest dreadnoughts was less than five miles.

Scheer had no option but to order another *Gefechtskehrtwendung*. This time, with the range being much closer, the British would easily spot what was happening and react accordingly. Therefore, before he gave the order to turn, he issued two others. The first was to Hipper, whose battlecruisers were midway between the two battle fleets. He was ordered to distract the British while the battle fleet escaped. In fact Hipper had just boarded a destroyer at the time, having left his crippled flagship *Lützow*. So it fell to *Kapitän* Hartog of the *Derfflinger* to lead the already damaged battlecruisers in what was later described as a suicidal 'death ride'. The battlecruisers were pounded badly, as was Behnke's Battle Squadron III, at the front of the German dreadnought line. To cover the withdrawal of both, Scheer ordered in his destroyers.

The signal 'Attack with Torpedoes' was made at 1921hrs, while the battle turn-away was already in progress. *Kommodore* Michelsen, commanding the fleet's torpedo boats, was two miles to the south of the fleet flagship at the time and had 13 boats at his disposal from Flotillas VI and IX. They immediately set off towards the British, their funnels belching thick black smoke. A minute

TORPEDO ATTACK: BATTLE OF JUTLAND, 1915–1925HRS

At a critical moment in the battle, when the German battle fleet found itself outmanoeuvred by their British opponents, *Vizeadmiral* Scheer sacrificed his battlecruisers and torpedo boats in order to save his dreadnoughts.

After the first encounter between the two battle fleets at Jutland *Vizeadmiral* Scheer broke contact, turning away from his opponent. He then led his fleet back towards the east, hoping to engage the British on more favourable terms. Instead, at 1900hrs, for the second time that day, he found himself crossing the 'T' of the British battle line – his dreadnoughts heading at right angles towards Admiral Jellicoe's British dreadnoughts, whose massed guns threatened to overwhelm the head of the German line.

Scheer ordered another *Gefechtskehrtwendung* ('Battle turn-away') to avoid the enemy's guns.

This time, though, with the range down to a few miles, he was still in grave danger. Therefore, he ordered *Kapitän* Hartog of *Derfflinger*, who was temporarily commanding the German battlecruisers, to distract the enemy. Surprisingly the battlecruisers, though battered, all survived what became known as 'Von Hartog's Death Ride'. To drive the British off, Scheer ordered in his torpedo boats. A massed torpedo attack might force the British dreadnoughts to break contact, and so give the German battle fleet a better chance to escape.

EVENTS

1. The German battle fleet runs away from the British dreadnoughts. Scheer orders *Kommodore* Heinrich in the light cruiser *Regensburg*, commanding the Scouting Forces' torpedo boats, to attack the British dreadnoughts.

2. Hartmann leads the German battlecruisers of Scouting Group I across the front of the German battle fleet, screening it from the British fire. Although the battlecruisers are badly hammered, they all survive the 'death ride'.

3. Heinrich's Flotillas VI and IX were deployed on the flank of the battle fleet. They advanced towards the enemy, passing astern of the German battlecruisers. *Regensburg* accompanied the destroyers but detached from them on reaching the line of the battlecruisers. As a command ship, *Regensburg* would take no direct part in the torpedo attack.

4. At 1921hrs, as the torpedo boats came within range, Scheer reiterated his order *Torpedoboote Ran!* ('Torpedo Boats Attack!'). Flotilla VI only had four boats available (G–41, V–44, G–87 and G–86), led by Kvtkpt Schultz in G–41, the Flottilleboot (flotilla leader).

5. G–41 was hit, and G–86 damaged by medium-calibre guns from the dreadnoughts, but the flotilla still managed to launch a spread of 11 torpedoes.

6. Seeing this, Jellicoe ordered his battle fleet to turn away from the enemy. This gave his ships the best possible chance of avoiding the torpedoes, but it risked breaking contact with the German battle fleet.

7. Flotilla XI, reduced to nine boats, also attacked Kvtkpt Goehle in Flotilleboot V–26, was accompanied by V–26, S–36, S–51, S–52, V–30, S–34, S–33 and S–35, although some of these had already expended several of their torpedoes. They launched 16 torpedoes. As the destroyers withdrew, they laid a thick smoke screen to cover their escape. S–35, however, was hit and sunk during the attack.

8. As the British battle fleet turned away, and the smoke screen now hid the German battle fleet, the two sides lost contact with each other. Only the British battlecruisers remained in a position to regain contact with the German fleet.

Although none of the German torpedoes hit their targets, there were several instances of near misses. Jellicoe had been lucky, but Scheer was more concerned that his diversion had worked. Thanks to the 'death ride' and the torpedo boat attack, the High Seas Fleet now had a chance of escaping intact.

German dreadnoughts

Fr. Der Grosse (Scheer)

German battlecruisers

Derfflinger (von Hartog)

Smoke screen

British dreadnoughts

Iron Duke (Jellicoe)

British battlecruisers

Lion (Beatty)

later, five more destroyers from Flotilla III joined in the attack. This forced the British dreadnoughts to stop firing at the German capital ships, and deal with this more immediate threat. The leading torpedo boat, flotilla leader *G-41*, took a direct hit, and slewed away, but the others raced on with shells falling all around them. Amazingly, only a handful of boats were hit during the torpedo attack.

Judging his moment, *Korvettenkapitän* Schultz, commanding the Flotilla VI, ordered his boats to launch their torpedoes. At that point, according to standing orders, they would then withdraw through their own smoke screen. The closest British ships were almost four miles away, so with hindsight this order was somewhat premature. That of course is easy to say when the attack appeared suicidal. Even the British were impressed by the courage of their assailants. As a petty officer on *Iron Duke* put it: 'I remember that German torpedo attack as the most exciting and bravest incident I saw at Jutland… It was the kind of dashing naval action prominent in boyish dreams.' To the north of Schultz's command was Flotilla IX, led by *Korvettenkapitän* Goehle. His own *V-28* took a hit and turned away, as did *S-51*, while alongside, *S-35* was ripped apart by a 15cm (6in) shell.

Still, between them these frail little boats of Flotillas VI and IX managed to launch a total of 31 torpedoes at the British dreadnoughts – 11 from Schultz's boats and the rest by Goehle's flotilla. Each of these boats carried six 50cm torpedoes, mounted in a mixture of twin and single launchers. Most boats had managed to fire off three, at a range of between three and five miles. These were fired in small batches, from around 1927hrs on, and aimed in the general direction of the British battle fleet. The German 50cm G6 torpedo had a range of 8,400m and a speed of 27 knots. That meant it could take over seven minutes to reach the closest British ships. The range also meant the British did not see the torpedoes being launched. It was only when the torpedo boats turned away that they realized they were in the water.

However, Jellicoe had already given his evasive orders at 1922hrs. The textbook reaction was to turn the ships away from the oncoming torpedoes.

German torpedo boats speed in to the attack at Jutland, in a detail of *Der Schlacht am Skaggerak* by Claus Bergen. However, this mass attack, carried out by three flotillas, was made at long range and achieved little. Nevertheless, it did force Jellicoe's battle fleet to break contact, and so helped cover the withdrawal of Scheer and Hipper's capital ships.

The advantages were obvious. Instead of a closing rate of 27 knots, this reduced the rate by the speed of the dreadnought, typically 20 knots, and it made it more likely the torpedoes would run out of their propellant before they reached their target. It also reduced the target area presented to the torpedoes, giving the dreadnoughts a fighting chance of escaping them. A number of British dreadnoughts endured near misses, but all of them emerged unscathed from the ordeal. Thanks to Jellicoe's quick reactions, none of his dreadnoughts had been hit.

It also meant that, in the excitement, he had lost contact with both the German battle fleet and the battlecruisers. The two fleets were now steaming in roughly opposite directions, while the growing area of sea between them was filled with funnel smoke, burning patches of wreckage and mist. The light was now fading, and while Scheer had not escaped past Jellicoe to the west, his fleet remained battered but intact. This second ambush by the British, albeit an unplanned one, had placed the German battle fleet in extreme danger for the second time. Scheer's quick reaction – ordering his battlecruisers to close with the enemy, before ordering another 'battle turn-away' – helped extricate the High Seas Fleet. It was only these two actions, combined with the mass torpedo boat attack, that finally ended the threat to the fleet. Taken together it summed up three things – the high-level of professionalism within the High Seas Fleet, the ability of the fleet to quickly communicate and respond to orders, and above all the courage of the crews, particularly in the battlecruisers and torpedo boats, both of whom were sent on what seemed at the time like a suicidal mission in order to save the bulk of their fleet. It was a moment when the men of the High Seas Fleet were put on trial. The way they responded was exemplary, and a credit to the *Kaiserliche Marine.*

ANALYSIS

In 1912, Churchill labelled the High Seas Fleet as a luxury fleet, created at immense cost in order to satisfy the ego of Kaiser Wilhelm II. There was certainly some truth in this, particularly as, with the benefit of hindsight, we know just how little this powerful naval force actually achieved. It can also be argued that the fleet itself was not the problem. It was the lack of any clear role that rendered it impotent, due in part to being thrust into a war for which it was ill-suited and equally ill-prepared.

The initial impetus behind the fleet was the Kaiser's will to create a naval force which gave him greater standing on the geopolitical stage. It was always more about the status that a battle fleet would bring him than the tangible impact such a fleet might have. Germany's naval expansion only gained momentum after 1897, when Admiral von Tirpitz launched the political campaign to fund it, and in the process he also had to justify it to the Reichstag. This was the source of the *Risikogedanke* 'risk theory' stratagem, the idea that the new battle fleet was a deterrent, which could (while sacrificing itself) cripple the power of the Royal Navy in battle. However, not only did Germany have no strategic naval partner in 1914 – the essential other half of the stratagem – but thanks to the Kaiser's proprietorial attitude towards his fleet, he was never prepared to sacrifice the High Seas Fleet in a naval war of attrition.

After the battle of Jutland both sides tried to make sense of the largest naval battle of the period, fought in misty conditions, where visibility was often obscured by funnel smoke. This German map is typical of the neatly produced efforts of both sides as they tried to find order in the various fleet movements that day.

This led to the adoption of the *Kräfteausgleich* 'force balancing' stratagem, which changed the whole aim of the High Seas Fleet. For this to succeed, it required four things. The first was a powerful Scouting Force, able to seek out segments of the enemy fleet, isolate them, then pin them until the German battle fleet could arrive to finish the job. Crucially, this also required other means of naval reconnaissance, such as signal intercepts, U-boats and Zeppelins to detect the enemy when they put to sea. This was never sufficient or effective enough for the task, and thanks to the Kaiser's desire for 'a place in the sun', many of the *Kaiserliche Marine*'s cruisers were overseas, protecting German colonies, and were not available to reinforce Hipper's Scouting Forces.

Kräfteausgleich also depended on the possession of a large force of ocean-going torpedo boats and U-boats, which were perfectly designed to target enemy capital ships. The High Seas Fleet had the destroyers, but from 1915 on, the U-boat flotillas were usually deployed elsewhere, fighting their own war against Allied merchant shipping. Consequently, for most of the time, very few of them were available for naval reconnaissance, or to specifically target the enemy battle fleet. In theory sea mines could help achieve the same purpose, but despite thousands being laid around the British coast, only the dreadnought *Audacious* was sunk by a mine, thereby altering the force balance of the battle fleets.

This led to the third factor – the actual naval balance. In his first decade in office Tirpitz had made great progress in building up a battle fleet, although it was still too small to challenge the British. When *Dreadnought* entered service in 1906, the clock was reset as all existing battleships were now obsolete, and both the British and the German navies had to start again from scratch. This threw Tirpitz's long-term plans into disarray, as dreadnoughts were hugely more expensive than pre-dreadnought battleships. Nevertheless, at the insistence of the Kaiser, Germany entered into a naval race with Britain. In 1911 the Royal Navy had 11 dreadnoughts in service, while the *Kaiserliche Marine* had seven. From 1912 on, though, the gap widened, and by August 1914 the British had 20 dreadnoughts in service, and the Germans had just 13 of them.

This gap widened further as the war continued. Despite the loss of *Audacious* in October 1914, by the time of Jutland in May 1916 the British had 30 operational dreadnoughts, including several new 'fast battleships' sporting 15in (38cm) guns. The High Seas Fleet only had 17 dreadnoughts, forcing *Vizeadmiral* Scheer to bulk out his fleet with six pre-dreadnoughts. As early as 1912 it was clear that Britain had won the naval arms race by a handsome margin, so even before the outbreak of war two years later, *Kräfteausgleich* had become almost impossibly hard to achieve. Jutland had reduced this stratagem to tatters. Rather than reducing the strength of the Grand Fleet, Scheer's own battle fleet had been lucky to survive. Consequently, from that point on, any hope of achieving *Kräfteausgleich* was abandoned.

This stratagem might have worked earlier in the war, if the commanders of the High Seas Fleet had been allowed to do their job. Instead, their ability to plan aggressive sorties and to develop a coordinated strategy for 'force balancing' was effectively removed by the Kaiser. His desire to protect 'his' battle fleet and, after the Dogger Bank action, the risk-averse rules of engagement he imposed, tied the hands of his fleet commanders. The bait to achieve any effective 'force balancing' would obviously require placing some part of the High Seas Fleet at risk. Most likely this would be Hipper's 1st Scouting Group, as it operated independently of

After the signing of the Armistice, one of the terms was the disarmament of the fleet and its surrender to the Allies. Here, ammunition is landed in preparation for the journey to the Firth of Forth, where *Vizeadmiral* Reuter was to surrender the fleet.

the battle fleet. The one time this baiting almost worked was during the opening phase of Jutland. When it failed, the German battle fleet itself almost ran into a trap set by Jellicoe.

The High Seas Fleet grew after Jutland by three new, powerful capital ships (*Bayern*, *Baden* and *Hindenburg*), but it was not enough to tip the naval balance, as the British added six battlecruisers to counter them. In 1917, the US Navy also reinforced the Grand Fleet with dreadnoughts of their own. The German fleet would sortie again after

On 21 November 1918, the major warships of the High Seas Fleet surrendered to the Allies off the Scottish coast. They were then escorted to Scapa Flow where they were interned. Manned by a skeleton crew, the warships remained there for several months, as peace talks dragged on in Versailles. Finally, to avoid the fleet becoming a prize of war, these crews simultaneously scuttled their ships on 21 June 1919. Here, the masts and funnels of the new battlecruiser *Hindenburg* are left sticking above the waters of Scapa Flow.

Jutland, but these operations became increasingly rare, as growing fuel shortages limited the ability of the fleet to put to sea. From that point on, the High Seas Fleet was reduced to something akin to a 'fleet in being', its only role being to tie down the Grand Fleet in the North Sea theatre for the remainder of the war, and to prevent an Allied amphibious invasion of the German coast. That only achieved the very limited aim that Jellicoe's fleet could not be deployed elsewhere, against Germany's Austro-Hungarian or Turkish allies.

Seen in these terms – the lack of an effective role and its strategic impotence – the High Seas Fleet represented a colossal waste of resources. In 1911–12, when the naval arms race was at its height, Germany spent almost 500 million gold marks a year on its navy. This was even larger than the budget allotted to the German army. With hindsight, the same strategic result might have been achieved in the North Sea if, instead of a powerful battle fleet, the *Kaiserliche Marine* had followed a more modest course, based around coastal defence. A combination of U-boats, destroyers, mines and coastal defence monitors could have achieved the same ends for a fraction of the cost. The Kaiser, though, wanted his fleet.

This said, until the final weeks of the war the High Seas Fleet remained a potent, powerful and highly professional force. Ship for ship its capital ships were as good as those of Jellicoe's Grand Fleet: although generally less well armed, they were more resilient to damage. The Bayerns, appearing towards the end of the war, were arguably the best capital ships of the period. The fleet was largely well led, and tactically it was as good as its opponent. Arguably, at Jutland it was the better handled, despite being outnumbered and outgunned. If the Kaiser had not been so overly protective of it, and if its commanders had been given a clear strategy, then the High Seas Fleet might have achieved much more than it did. If *Kräfteausgleich* had actually succeeded – to paraphrase Churchill's famous quote about Jellicoe – it might even have been able to end the war in an afternoon.

FURTHER READING

Campbell, John, *Jutland: An Analysis of the Fighting* (Conway Maritime Press, London, 1998)

Freidman, Norman, *Naval Firepower: Battleship Guns and Gunnery in the Dreadnought Era* (Seaforth Publishing, Barnsley, 2008)

Freidman, Norman, *Naval Weapons of World War One: An Illustrated Directory* (Seaforth Publishing, Barnsley, 2011)

Freidman, Norman, *Fighting the Great War at Sea: Strategy, Tactics and Technology* (Seaforth Publishing, Barnsley, 2014)

Gardiner, Robert (ed.), *Conway's All the World's Fighting Ships, 1860–1905* (Conway Maritime Press, London, 1979)

Gardiner, Robert (ed.), *Conway's All the World's Fighting Ships, 1906–1921* (Conway Maritime Press, London, 1985)

Gardiner, Robert (ed.), *The Eclipse of the Big Gun: The Warship, 1906–45*; Conway's History of the Ship Series (Conway Maritime Press, London, 1992)

Gröner, Erich, *German Warships, 1815–1945: Vol. 1 Major Surface Vessels* (Conway Maritime Press, London, 1982)

Halpern, Paul G., *A Naval History of World War 1* (Naval Institute Press, Annapolis MD, 1994)

Hansen, Hans Jürgen, *The Ships of the German Fleets, 1848–1945* (Naval Institute Press, Annapolis MD, 1988)

Herwig, Holger H., *Luxury Fleet: The Imperial German Navy, 1888–1918* (George Allen & Unwin Ltd, London, 1980)

Hodges, Peter, *The Big Gun: Battleship Main Armament 1860–1945* (Conway Maritime Press, London, 1981)

Jane, Fred T. (ed.), *Fighting Ships – 1914* (David & Charles Ltd, Newton Abbot, 1968; first published 1914)

Jane, Fred T. (ed.), *Jane's Fighting Ships of World War 1* (Random House Group, London, 2001; first published 1919)

Jellicoe, Nicholas, *Jutland: The Unfinished Battle* (Seaforth Publishing, Barnsley, 2016)

Konstam, Angus, *Jutland 1916: Twelve Hours to Win the War* (Aurum Press, London, 2016)

Le Fleming, H. M., *Warships of World War 1*, 4 vols (Ian Allen, Hampton Court, 1961)

London, Charles, *Jutland 1916: Clash of the Dreadnoughts* (Osprey Publishing, Oxford, 2000)

Massie, Robert, *Dreadnought: Britain, Germany and the Coming of the Great War* (Jonathan Cape, London, 1992)

Perrett, Bryan, *North Sea Battleground: The War at Sea, 1914–18* (Pen & Sword, Barnsley, 2015)

Ruge, Friedrich, *Scapa Flow 1919: The End of the German Fleet* (Ian Allan, English edition, London, 1973; first published in German, 1969)

Scheer, Reinhard, *Germany's High Seas Fleet in the First World War* (Pen & Sword, Barnsley, 2014; first published London, 1920)

Schleihauf, William (ed.), *Jutland: The Naval Staff Appreciation* (Seaforth Publishing, Barnsley, 2016)

Staff, Gary, *German Battlecruisers of World War One: Their Design, Construction and Operations* (Seaforth Publishing, Barnsley, 2014)

Wolz, Nicolas, *From Imperial Splendour to Internment: The German Navy in the First World War* (Seaforth Publishing, Barnsley, 2020)

Woodward, David, *The Collapse of Power: Mutiny in the High Seas Fleet* (Arthur Baker Ltd, London, 1973)

INDEX

Page references in **bold** *refer to an illustration; n to a note.*